To: Elizabeth

Best wish

Robert M. Thompson

MW00815571

Wisdom, Apples
& Black Roses

Wisdom, Apples & Black Roses

Robert M. Thompson

www.ivyhousebooks.com

All quotes not identified by an author are original quotes
by Robert M. Thompson.

PUBLISHED BY IVY HOUSE PUBLISHING GROUP
5122 Bur Oak Circle, Raleigh, NC 27612
United States of America
919-782-0281
www.ivyhousebooks.com

ISBN 13: 978-1-57197-484-6
Library of Congress Control Number: 2007933459

Printed in the United States of America

Table of Contents

Foreword

Wisdom, Apples and Black Roses is a delightful and thought-provoking first book by Bob Thompson. I hope there are more to follow.

I had the good fortune to meet Bob during the early stages of his writing and, over the years, to enjoy occasional discussions of his development and organization of ideas. He has drawn from a lifetime of observing people closely, talking with them and getting to know the character of wisdom. From reading Bob's draft manuscripts, and now this finished work, I am impressed by the faithfulness of his words to his philosophy and the clarity with which he shares them.

Bob's style is one of guiding and offering instruction—never of lecturing. To lecture would be at complete odds with his message. He offers many of his ideas through storytelling—a communication form that once allowed generations to pass on their heritage and to convey the thread of long-tested wisdom in a personalized and familiar environment. You'll find these interesting; and you may read through them quickly at first, more slowly the next time and go back to them after you've read new ones in the subsequent chapters. These are stories you can read separately to your children and other younger ones as a way to share your own personal wisdom and understanding of life with them.

This is indeed an enjoyable book to read in one sitting, or a chapter at a time, and to reread as one journeys towards a clearer appreciation and applies that understanding to the choices made in day-to-day living. One day, perhaps, you'll find yourself clutching a fistful of black roses!

—KEN INGOLD
June 2007

Preface

This volume is intended to introduce the reader to wisdom, one of the most misunderstood life-changing forces in the universe. The power of wisdom, unlike knowledge and common sense, is given only to those who truly and deeply desire it. The findings and examples presented herein are the result of more than thirty years of observations and interviews. I have gotten to know people who appear to possess the kind of wisdom that propelled them to levels far beyond the masses. Subjects were interviewed informally through relaxed and friendly conversations without their even knowing the purpose of my inquiries. Over the last quarter-century plus, my casual research has involved people from almost every state, occupation, race, economic status, age and, of course, a fair mixture of men and women. In addition, I interviewed men and women from Asia, Europe, Africa, South America and the Middle East. I was fortunate enough to live in Europe for almost two years and to spend time in eight different countries. I must, however, confess my conversations were with only those who could speak my language. I found the wise were always willing to exchange ideas and were always courteous.

I learned that wisdom cannot be taught and passed on to others, but the ways of the wise can be. It is my desire to present the reader with knowledge concerning the nature of wisdom and how one approaches wisdom. Through the use of anecdotes, I have given examples of how the wise make decisions and face life's issues. My goal is to encourage readers to understand wisdom and to pursue it on their own.

Chapter One
Wisdom and Apples

Wisdom is more precious than jewels, and nothing you desire can compare to it.
         —Proverbs 3:15 (Revised Standard Version)

Tom, a rising senior at State University, had just arrived at the office of his advisor to plan his curriculum for the coming year. The school required that each student meet with their advisor upon completing his or her junior year to ensure they would be adequately enrolled for the necessary subjects to qualify for a degree in their major. As Tom waited to be called into his conference, he wondered about his last three years and questioned if he was truly prepared to move into his senior year of study. He wondered, if at the end of that year, he would feel as inadequately prepared as he did now. Had he learned, at this point of his studies, what others at his same level of achievement knew? As he waited, his doubts increased.

Finally, Tom was called in for the interview. The advisor was an elderly gentleman slightly past the age where most professors retire, but he was very much in tune with his younger students. He was admired by his students and faculty alike for his wisdom and unique problem-solving abilities. The interview began with a review of Tom's previous three years of study, which were quite successful in terms of grade point average and knowledge of assigned material. After discussing the next year's schedule, the professor asked Tom how he felt about his own progress since entering the university. "Sir, I admire your wisdom, and I thought that after three years of college I would have at least gained some wisdom of my own by now; but I do not find that to be the case. Can you tell me how to gain wisdom, the kind that you seem to have mastered? Maybe I don't understand wisdom, but I know it's not coming from my studies, even though my grades are superior. Is there something you can recommend I study or read that will show me how to gain wisdom?"

After listening to Tom's questions and concerns the wise old professor thought for a few moments before responding. Finally he said, "Tom, for a long time I have watched you walk to class each morning carrying an apple, which I assume you eat during the day. I'm sure by now you have eaten hundreds of apples while on campus, but what can you tell me about those apples? Do you understand their commercial significance or their uses in promoting good health or still the beneficial by-products of the apple? Do you know anything about their geographical distributions, their botanical makeup or the number and variety of apples available?" To these questions Tom could only confirm his ignorance of the subject of apples.

The professor then issued a challenge to the young student. "Tom," he said, "I think I can give you an assignment for the summer that will help you understand wisdom if you are willing to give it your time and effort. While you are out of school for the summer, take the subject of your apple and research all the data you can find about apples. Attack the subject from all possible angles from planting of the seed to its final destination, which can be the family table, or the manufacture of its by-products. When you return to campus next fall with your completed report, bring it by my office where I will then read it and set an appointment time for us to discuss it in detail. I know you don't at this time understand how this ties into your concerns about gaining wisdom, but if you will accept this challenge I'm sure you will find it helpful." Tom agreed to the challenge and began thinking about how he could fit the project into his summer activities.

It was a busy summer for Tom, but his three years of college had taught him how to organize his time and do detailed research. He utilized all the resources available at his local library, and then went to the Internet before finally ordering pamphlets from the Apple Growers Association. The most surprising and interesting part of his research was when he found an overwhelming amount of data on shipping, preserving and preparing apples for commercial use, especially in the fermentation and distillation of vinegar. What seemed to Tom to be a real chore for the summer became an enjoyable and enlightening venture.

The long summer finally ended, and Tom found himself back on campus anxious to schedule a meeting with his advisor. Little did he know that his advisor, "the wise old professor," was just as anxious to see Tom and find out how his research was progressing. At last they were face-to-face with the large volume of research on the desk between them. After a few minutes of small talk about their summer activities, the advisor suggested that Tom give him a week to review the material and at the end of the week meet again to discuss it. After all, both were busy getting settled into the new school year.

The following week the interview resumed with compliments to Tom about his report. The professor begin his critique with, "Tom, I have reviewed your report which I conclude is perhaps the most thorough essay written by an undergraduate on any subject. You learned from your study of apples their economic importance to a global economy as well as their commercial uses. You seem to understand the pharmacological value of the apple, it's by-products, and how they are prepared and preserved. Your knowledge of how apples require constant care to prevent them from becoming diseased is extensive. Also stated in your report are the types of soils and climates required for the various varieties of apples. You show the chemical changes an apple makes in its ripening process along with its overall chemical make-up. The geographical distribution and shipping problems, you seem to understand quite well. Another strong point in your report is your understanding of the botanical make-up of the apple, and you even know the average number of seeds in each variety of apple. So, at this point, I only have one question for you. Can you tell me how many apples there are in a seed?"

Tom was caught by surprise and remained silent for several moments contemplating the question he never expected. Finally, he responded, "No sir, only God knows that." The professor then smiled at Tom and politely said, "Tom, you just had your first lesson in wisdom. For to be wise is to know where our knowledge and wisdom stop and where God's continues. With all the effort and time you spent on your report, there will be questions that are beyond your ability to answer. The wise know this and are humbled by it. In order to be wise, you must experience humility. Remember, it was Wise Men who humbled themselves to kneel in a humble setting to pay tribute to someone they perceived to be greater than themselves. Wisdom is not a lofty status, but a humbling experience; and the first jewel in the crown of wisdom is humility."

Why do people from the same background, family, home or school solve the same problems and challenges differently? Some will approach tasks at hand with calm assurance while others worry over the solution before even trying. Still others will shy away without ever facing their problem. People may have the same level of education and the same level of intelligence, but the basic difference in their approach is wisdom. Based on my observations and research, only about five to seven percent of the population truly masters the ideals of wisdom. No one profession, color, creed or sex has a monopoly on wisdom. Wisdom does not abound in the halls of academia, great medical institutions or institutions of religion in any significant ratios than from other professions. The same is true in government, politics and journalism. These professions, because of their high profiles, provide most of the information we receive throughout our lives; but we should never assume it all comes from wisdom. It comes from technical knowledge or specialized knowledge, which can be perceived as a substitute for wisdom.

The ratio of five to seven percent is supported by at least four authors: Earl Nightingale, the authors of *Royal Path of Life* (p. 238), T.L. Haines and L.W. Yaggy, and William H. Danforth, author of *I Dare You* (p. 105). They never describe their five percent as having wisdom but in their description of these individuals the characteristics they cite are those of the wise. Even though the percentage is small in those mastering wisdom, there seems to be a common trait among these special people. They all started with a hunger to find something that truly satisfied, and they found it in wisdom. The hunger usually starts with a mere wish for wisdom, which later graduates itself into desire and then hunger. A crescendo of emotion takes place, and the hunger eventually is satisfied—wisdom being the final result. This process is not instantaneous and usually takes years. There is never a given moment when you suddenly feel wisdom is achieved; but you may be aware of being wiser today than in years past. Humility never allows the wise to admit and boast about their wisdom.

Who are these people we call wise? They are the ones you seek in times of crises. They are the ones you will remember after the parties are over even though they may not have been the most physically attractive, but were by far the most interesting. The wise are rich with friendships and respect from others. They are sought out by others who are lonely and in need of advice and compassion.

The philosopher Zeno and the Stoics believed the wise should be without emotions such as passion, joy and grief. Today some people still believe this but I do not find to be true. I concede, however, they do put their emotions aside when making difficult decisions, but they live by far the most exciting and rewarding lives of anyone on the planet. It is with dignity and grace they experience the height of their joys, the depth of their grievances, and the excitement of their passions.

The wise can be found in every country, every religion, every race and in both sexes. I, like most others, always assumed that wisdom belonged to the elderly and was acquired with age, but I was wrong. There were two teenage girls in my community who proved to me that wisdom can start from a very early age. Both of these girls are now adults with children of their own and are still "real ladies." My thanks to Jennifer and Janice for their examples.

Wisdom is available to any person, anywhere, who desires it. To desire and obtain wisdom, it is essential to understand that the power of God and the universe is equally present in all places, at all times, and is available to everyone. This power comes to us in the form of wisdom. It is a goal anyone can seek. In seeking wisdom, it is also necessary to be open to the messages of the universe and God. There are four phases in mastering wisdom: 1) practice humility; 2) develop an acute level of awareness; 3) become more courageous in facing daily decisions and 4) learn to be content. These phases are also known as the four jewels in the crown of wisdom.

As this volume unfolds, you will be shown each of the four jewels in the crown of wisdom and will learn that wisdom as it comes to us is without error. To keep it error free, we will learn further that ego, prejudice, pride and self serving agendas must be controlled or sacrificed. Because knowledge can have error, you must be willing to seriously question and perhaps discard many of your most cherished beliefs. This may be true only for those whose lives are out of control and who have practiced a life of being closed-minded. Chances are those who seek wisdom will receive a new and elevated meaning to the beliefs and lifestyle they already have. Wisdom reveals inconsistencies between our actions and beliefs for the purpose of allowing us to choose what elevates us to greatness.

Chapter Two
The Crown of Wisdom

Wisdom will place on your head a fair garland; she will bestow on you a beautiful crown.

—Proverbs 4:9 (RSV)

To wear the crown of wisdom, you must exemplify the standards and characteristics represented by its four jewels: humility, awareness, courage and contentment. In varying degrees, you may experience moments of your own wisdom; but to wear the crown, wisdom must rule every moment of your life and encompass body, mind and soul as one. Your journey must begin with enough humility to at least start controlling your ego. This is essential for moving to the next step: awareness. If the ego is not harnessed, your prejudices will always overshadow the messages you need to be receiving for your journey to wisdom.

Humility

Don't let your ego speak to you so loudly you can't hear the messages sent your way for building wisdom.

Humility is all about controlling the ego. It is the first jewel in the crown of wisdom and is perhaps more difficult to understand than all the other three. Unfortunately, the most popular concept of humility is that it mirrors weakness, self-depreciation and submissive behavior. We seldom associate humility with courage, strength, boldness and firmness of will, but any reference to humility in this writing will represent these characteristics. Weakness is never a part of wisdom, but is always exposed by wisdom. Practicing humility is the first step in seeking wisdom. The art of practicing humility does not have to be completely mastered before wisdom becomes your goal.

Wisdom is life's most perfect gift to mortals. It is ignored by the masses, scorned by many and embraced by few. It comes from God and the universe without error. It can only be a life-changing force if we refuse to contaminate it with our own pride and prejudices. Pride and prejudice in no way ever advance the ideals of wisdom. The wise believe that God is equally present in all places at all times and, therefore, must be equally present in all people regardless of their sex, age, location and race. This does not change even when we recognize that our gifts and talents are not the same.

True humility teaches us that we are never superior or inferior to any other person, but we are always less than God. Humility is the only thing that can cleanse our vessel (self) to receive pure and untarnished messages from God and the universe. Remember, it was the Wise Men who humbled themselves by traveling long distances to bow down in a humble setting before a baby believed to be divine and holy. At the same time, they defied an earthly king who had the power to destroy them—a perfect example of how humility and courage can work together. The Wise Men had status, power and wealth, but they put these aside and became "poor in spirit" while seeking something greater than themselves. This does not imply they relinquished their wealth and power, but rather they lowered the importance of these for something higher. In doing so, they solidified their status as "Wise Men."

In dealing with the affairs of life, the wise rely on logic and reason. True logic and reason cannot exist where prejudices, pride, hate or any other negative emotion dominates one's thinking. Even positive emotions may have to be put aside when making difficult decisions. With humility as the catalyst, decisions are made by great men and women on the basis of what serves the greatest good for the greatest number. In the midst of unpopular crises, the wise are called on to discard their own feelings and preferences. An excellent example is how Winston Churchill dealt with decisions, unpopular even to himself, to bring the war (WWII) effort to its successful conclusion.

Decisions that are often unpopular can isolate the wise from others, but can set them far above the masses in their understanding—knowing, of course, that popular decisions are not necessarily the right ones. Isolating one's self is not new to the wise. To obtain wisdom through humility, the wise mentally, spiritually and sometimes bodily must have their own "desert" experience. Even Jesus, Mohammed, Buddha and others had to face themselves in a lonely setting. This lonely setting does not necessarily have to be a physical location, but can be anywhere as long as you are willing to set yourself aside and deal with personal "demons" and temptations. Stories come from men and women who had desert experiences on hospital beds, in prisons or even at home in the midst of broken or abusive marriages.

As emphasized in the biblical story of Jesus' desert experience, there were three temptations he overcame on his road to humility by setting aside his own selfish will. One temptation he faced was personal security—turning the stones into bread. The second temptation was power promised him by worshipping someone or something other than God. The third temptation he faced was sensationalism—throwing himself down for the sake of tempting God. Sensationalism can and often does present itself as hedonism. Hedonism is the doctrine that pleasure is the sole chief good in life and that moral duty is fulfilled in the gratification of pleasure seeking instincts and dispositions (*Webster's Collegiate Dictionary, 2nd Edition*). These three temptations must be faced by anyone who seeks wisdom. Putting these in their proper prospective removes them from the path that leads to humility.

Another pathway to humility is through self-denial. In ancient times, and in some cultures, people believed their gods demanded sacrifice, which was often given out of fear. The ultimate sacrifice was even their healthiest child and in the case of young girls, virgins. Some cultures were not so extreme in practicing self-denial, but showed some signs that it was part of their basic belief. Going back in time to early Jewish history, Abraham sacrificed animals by burning them on a self-made altar, believing it was required by God but not understanding why. Why would a loving God want him to give up something he worked for, and besides, what would God need with a burnt animal or the smoke from burning it? The truth is he didn't need either; but to understand sacrifice, you have to look at the way society was structured in Abraham's time.

In those days, adult children of families often lived with their aged parents, their siblings, spouses of siblings, their own spouses and children, nieces and nephews. All worked as a unit by providing their food and clothing. They made many of their own tools and weapons when possible and would barter for others, which often meant a day's travel or more to a trading post. As a self-sufficient unit, the family had limited contacts with others—unless on rare occasions travelers passed through their territory. Servants and concubines were part of the family unit, often referred to as a tribe or clan. With everyone in the household well taken care of, there was little concern about interacting with others on the outside. So the idea of humility and self-denial was of little consequence. When Abraham felt the call of God to offer sacrifices, the most logical course was to give up something of value. Little did he realize his practice would be handed down for generations but would be misunderstood. Few people understood then or understand now that sacrifice is a discipline in self-denial. For the kind of society that was to evolve, complex relationships would require wisdom. For wisdom to evolve, humility had to be instilled into traditions and beliefs with self-denial as its cornerstone.

Awareness

All growth and personal achievement is in direct proportion to the amount of truth we can take about ourselves.

Awareness, the second jewel in the crown of wisdom, takes you to the highest level possible of being in tune to God and the universe. Without awareness, personal growth is impossible; without personal growth, wisdom can never be achieved. Thus, it is important that we be truthful with ourselves and not try to filter messages we receive from the universe through our egos (see previous section on Humility for controlling ego). Awareness makes it possible to identify landmarks on the roadway to wisdom and gauge one's progress or lack of it. It holds up to us information concerning where we are physically, mentally and emotionally at all times. One of the very basic elements in map reading is to know where we are on the map before we can determine what corrections are necessary to reach our destination. Awareness also gives us information about those around us. Awareness tells us when those near us are in need, in trouble or are causing problems and danger to others.

There are two excellent teachers the universe has given man for his striving to achieve wisdom. They are adversity and consequence. Adversity is the least welcome of the two and can appear without invitation. Examples of adversity are accidents, disease and natural disasters. Each of these, although not necessarily sent to give you a lesson, often provides to the wise an opportunity to make life-changing decisions and realign priorities. You most often don't have a choice as to your adversities, but you always have a choice through free will as to how you react to those adversaries. You will seldom react to what is happening to you, but you always react to how you perceive what is happening to you. When adversity teaches that change is needed, a heightened sense of awareness is required to bring about that change. Consequences, on the other hand, are always invited, but not always consciously invited. The actions and decisions you choose send out invitations to the consequences compatible with your choices. To take away your consequence is to deny you the opportunity to learn and grow in wisdom. This concept is extremely important in training children to become good citizens. Taking away consequences from children sends signals that rules of good behavior and manners are not important and are not necessary to follow. If taken to the extreme, these signals can encourage sociopathic tendencies. Likewise, to remove penalties for wrongdoing promotes injustice.

Eliminating unfavorable consequences builds character; avoiding unfavorable consequences destroys character.

Every concept we adopt about ourselves and our lifestyle leaves an indelible mark that can provide a lesson to us through awareness. How we dress, how we vote, how we take care of our body, the cars we drive, the friends we choose, the way we wear our hair, the places we choose to go (or not go) for spiritual guidance, all are indications of who we are. These characteristics can be read back like a recorded journal to help us move into a higher plane of understanding and move closer to wisdom. This whole process may seem complicated, but in reality, it is the easiest thing you can do since the only requirement for gaining wisdom is to earnestly desire it and be willing to listen for messages from God (or the universe) with humility. As noted in the previous section, humility is the key to not distorting the lessons we receive.

To those who want to learn how to read the messages they receive, it is suggested that they start with the six physical senses. To refresh our memories, the six physical senses are: 1) taste, 2) smell, 3) sight, 4) hearing, 5) touch and 6) kinesthetic awareness (kinesthesia is how we experience gravity and weight of objects). To understand wisdom, you must accept the fact that mind, physical body and spirit form one unified personality. The mental processes determine what we choose to believe and how we wish to react to our choices. As this pattern is repeated, a belief system is established. By constantly repeating these beliefs, they become the cornerstones of one's spiritual make-up. Mental and spiritual planes then work together to control how we react on the physical plane. Clean thoughts and clean habits always produce clean actions. Evil thoughts and habits always produce evil ways. The beginning of evil thoughts most often are the result of an out-of-control ego.

Humility is the first step in controlling the ego and must be closely followed by an elevated awareness. Wisdom can never take place without cleansing ourselves of those belief patterns that interfere with receiving messages from God (or the universe). However, it is not necessary to totally master humility before reaching for a heightened sense of awareness. Awareness can help you reach an acceptable level of humility and, also, humility can help you reach an acceptable level of awareness.

Those who achieve a high level of awareness will always be aware of how choices made by others are affecting their own behavior, but awareness is not given just to judge others. Awareness is given to show us ways others react to life's circumstances and serve as an example for our own behavior. When we find the choices and lifestyles of others out of control, it may be a signal that our own lifestyles and choices need monitoring. If, on the other hand, we see positive results enjoyed by another, it then sets an example for those seeking a high level of awareness.

To be acutely aware gives the wise the ability to perceive when others are in need, suffering loss, lonely or having health issues. They can be an inspiration to others especially if they are open to sharing some of their experiences. The wise, who are always free-spirited, will attract others to them when they share what they themselves have overcome. Their message will show living as a free spirit did not evolve trouble free.

Not only are the wise acutely aware of the needs of others, they also monitor their own needs and habits essential for good physical health. Through awareness, body weights normalize and self-induced illnesses that are caused by bad habits are eliminated. Examples of these are: excessive obesity, smoking, excessive alcohol consumption, being unclean, stress and not getting enough rest. A heightened level of awareness can eliminate the need to ever go on a diet for excessive weight loss. Of course, there are conditions that occur within one's own body for which you have no control such as heredity and pollution. However, your body will always respond to your internal thoughts and decisions.

The benefits of being acutely aware are usually obvious, but there is one benefit that is often overlooked. Awareness gives you the ability to see humor in many of life's circumstances. If you have the ability to sense tragedy, loss, etc., then you also have the capacity to sense humor. Humor to the wise is not crude, hurtful to others or mean-spirited. Humor that is designed to degrade others (as is often found in political talk) or to make fun of physical traits (race, sex, height, deformities, etc.) does not come from the mouths of the wise. The wise not only find and see humor, but also can create it. By taking an ordinary message and giving it a literal meaning, not originally intended in its use, the outcome can be funny. For example: signs in store windows or highway signs can contain humor. If you would like to see and experience more humor in your life, printed signs are a good place to start since they can be done alone. Examples are signs in store windows, highway signs, and billboards and signs in businesses such as banks and restaurants. These are simple examples that show how, through awareness, the ordinary can bring a smile to one's face. Without awareness, wisdom is impossible. Enjoy it and make it fun as well as useful.

Courage

Fear is the beginning of courage.

Courage, the third jewel in the crown of wisdom, is perhaps the most misunderstood. If you have any intention of obtaining wisdom, courage must be understood and mastered. It is more than just valor. Those in civilized societies may never face life-threatening dangers that require bravery or resolve in battle and, therefore, conclude having courage is of little importance. The philosopher Plutarch said: "Courage consists not in hazarding without fear, but by being resolute in a just cause." (Haines and Yaggy, p. 215)

The noblest goal of courage is to move oneself from the status of being a victim to that of being a strong, free and unfettered decision maker. When something happens in our lives that brings about a temporary defeat, we are given choices. We can consider ourselves a victim and choose to remain so, or we can muster up enough courage to break out of the victim cycle. Since victims are not expected to exercise responsibility; they find it safe and comfortable to stay in victim status. They are like the Israelites who, during the Exodus, "longed for Egypt." In Egypt the Israelites knew what to expect even though they did not like it. It was easier for them to live in their days of victimhood than to have courage to face a new, freer life.

Even though courage is the force that changes lives, it must be tempered with purpose and discipline. Purpose and discipline are to courage as carbon is to steel. With courage tempered by purpose and discipline, goals move from dreams and wishes to their physical reality. Those who make wisdom a daily part of their life know the difference between dreaming and desiring. Dreaming is a feeble attempt at wanting without putting forth effort. It is true that all real goals start with a dream but must move into a state of real desire. Desire, the second stage of goal setting, must then be mixed with emotion—the kind of emotion that creates an excitement and hunger to succeed. If desire to succeed reaches an emotional level sufficient enough to create a "white heat" of anticipation, failure is never an option. Again, we may never be asked to do physical battle or to be a martyr unto death; but courage to achieve goals should be just as intense.

Courage is required not only for reaching goals but also for setting them. The wise recognize the difference between illusional goals and those that are real and noble. Students, for example, may set goals of only getting good grades for the purpose of pleasing their parents or qualifying for future employment. This is an example of an illusional goal that may only lead to the student's downfall through bad habits of cheating and plagiarism or bribery. The temptation to take short-cuts in obtaining goals that are not real is overwhelming and are in opposition to the moral codes of the wise. The noblest goal for any student would be to determine to learn everything the given course has to offer. In this way the student assures himself or herself of being prepared for any eventuality. Setting noble goals eliminates error and removes the temptation to do wrong. Noble goals, when achieved, often promote the achievement of lesser goals such as fame, fortune or good grades.

You should never confuse courage as being without humility. You will find humility is not weakness but is rather a courage within itself. It is the courage to control one's own ego for the purpose of understanding and receiving wisdom in its purest form without perverting it.

Without question, the most difficult test of courage is when you feel the need to stand alone and risk ridicule. Young men and women always desire to be included in the most popular circles and events, but some know they have thoughts and goals that are foreign to others. This should never mean something is wrong with them or their ideas. It probably implies they are thinking on a higher level and feel isolated from others who are not interested or maybe not capable of understanding. They then must decide whether to follow a different path at he risk of losing touch with a few friends or to muster up enough courage to endure. Unfortunately, many of these young subjects abandon dreams and cherished thoughts in favor of being popular. At these critical junctions, it would be beneficial to have an adult, steeped in wisdom, come to their rescue. A wise man or woman can help young minds understand the importance of treasuring thoughts and dreams without selling out to popularity. The wise also understand the art of social skills and can teach you how to reach a higher level of popularity and self respect through courage.

Courage does and must come into play in all day-to-day decisions. It can change the very fabric of society and eliminate many of the ills faced by civilization in the twenty-first century. Using pregnancy, for example, it takes courage to face the responsibility of raising children and assume the role of parent. It takes no courage to have an abortionist relieve one of that responsibility, especially if partial-birth is involved. The wise know there may be times when abortion is necessary based on medical considerations, but should not be used for the cowardly purpose of avoiding an inconvenience.

Further, courage is required in caring for the well being of future generations. It is amazing how many parents leave the education of their own children to educators. It takes courage to guide young minds. If more attention were given to providing a learning environment at home for school age children, there would be little or no need for special programs to aid children at risk. If parents would show courage by giving children proper instruction in avoiding irresponsible behavior, there would be little need for much of the legislation passed for protection from inanimate objects. For example, children can learn, with the help of responsible parents, to respect drugs, alcohol, firearms and tobacco. Instead it is easier and more cowardly to have government pass laws when parents know these things will never pass away. It would be far better for each child to know how to live responsibly in a world where these things are common. Just because there are drugs available, you do not have to use them. Just because there is alcohol in the house, it does not have to be drunk by minors. Just because there is a firearm in the house doesn't mean someone has to shoot it or feel threatened. The same logic is true for tobacco and its uses. Millions of children live around these things daily, but have not been trained to act responsibly towards dangerous inanimate objects.

Courage is absolutely essential in following through on projects and goals. Examples of gigantic tragedies and failures are recorded each day because someone failed to exercise courage in their decision making. We have all heard stories of those who cowardly avoid tasks essential to the achievement of a goal because it was too difficult, or they did not have the courage to develop skills necessary for achieving its final results. Sometimes it takes courage to do that which we do not enjoy but know is necessary. We like certain parts of our work and tend to do them first, ignoring those we don't like. Since both are essential, the job is usually half done or done in a sloppy way. I once had a client who I often convinced to include certain practices in developing and marketing his products. Once convinced, his first reaction was "let's do it now." As a result, this person always enjoyed his work and was successful beyond measure. A few years later, after his business was sold, he asked me to be a character reference on his application to enter the civil service. I was glad to be a witness to his courage and wisdom.

Contrast this story with the one about the student (Bill) who didn't like math, a person I also knew and had close contact with for many years.

I didn't know Bill when he was a young, but he always recounted stories of how he struggled with studies involving math. On days when he would have math tests, Bill would become violently sick and try to avoid attending school that day. The pressure to pass a required subject became so intense that Bill saw no other solution but to drop out of school. His parents and teachers always knew he was quite intelligent but exhibited no flair for working with numbers. They attributed his problem to his being unwilling to try; but as Bill later admitted to me, it was his lack of courage and his fear of failing. He had unparalleled courage in other areas and later became a decorated war hero.

As a young teenager, Bill spent much of his spare time reading stories of airplanes—how they were built for their particular function in wartime, their capabilities, speed and design. There was probably no airplane in Bill's time he could not identify and draw in exact detail. His goal was to work in an airplane factory and produce these "graceful beauties," as he referred to them. He would have loved to be involved in their design. Bill's problem was he didn't have the training to even be considered for employment in aircraft construction. Thus, he became bitter for having given up on his dream and daily blamed himself for his cowardliness of not putting forth enough effort to learn even the simplest forms of math.

One day Bill, now in his early forties, decided to at least learn how to fly and stay close to his love of airplanes. He signed up for flight training at a local airfield and soon discovered his written exam for obtaining a pilot's license would require more than just a basic understanding of math. There would be calculations for weight/load factors, course corrections based on wind speed and direction, time in transit based on Greenwich time and charting flight plans. He was so resolute in his determination he made up his mind to learn all the math required to become a licensed pilot. When he would have difficulty understanding a mathematical concept regarding his flight training, his flying buddies at the airfield would gladly help. Bill passed the written tests successfully, handled the in-flight calculations on each of his three solo cross-country flights and amazingly discovered he enjoyed math. To this day, he regrets his lack of courage in not tackling a problem well within his ability. Unless these lessons are understood and courage is given its proper place, wisdom will be unattainable.

Courage, like awareness and humility, helps the wise to eliminate unpleasant consequences by making the right decisions, or, learn from the consequences that do occur. Either of these courses of action give further proof to the wise that ethical behavior based on truth and virtue is the only pathway to follow.

Contentment

The wise are their own peacemakers. They make peace with themselves first.

Contentment, the fourth and final jewel in the crown of wisdom, reflects the ideals of the other three jewels. These ideals, once mastered, form the most coveted lifestyle and spiritual achievement known to mortals. Contentment was the goal great spiritual teachers of the past encouraged followers to seek. All five major religions were started with leaders who knew there was a connection between mortals and the world beyond their understanding. Their journey began with a hunger to make that connection. The first step was to become humble by recognizing the existence of something greater than themselves. The next step was to become aware of imperfections of the physical and the perceived perfection of immortal existence. The next obvious step was to have the necessary courage to initiate life-changing behavior for themselves and their followers. They did this by sharing their understanding of the standards set by an infinite world that is without error. Once achieved, contentment replaced chaos and order replaced confusion. This total process is known as wisdom, and those who have endured the test receive the crown of wisdom with its four jewels.

Contentment is the peace that calms spirit, mind and body. Contentment is to the mind as health is to the body. It promotes mental and physical health. Contentment should not be confused with serenity. Serenity is only the outward expression of contentment. Without contentment, serenity is temporary and fleeting.

As you express your contentment through serenity, you will be led to places and circumstances where grace, elegance, manners, virtue and peace abound. To the shallow of mind and the naive, peace is a word that describes only the absence of war or absence of armed conflict; but to the wise, it implies the absence of a troubled heart. In this context the heart is referred to as the very inner core of our being and not the organ that carries blood throughout the body. The wise know even in the absence of armed conflict around the world there would still be no peace on earth. There are still too many troubled hearts among men, women and children who need encouragement and care. Wisdom can bring peace to the suffering and encouragement to the needy, but there is a major problem. There is only a small percentage of people who achieve true wisdom in its highest form. As previously noted, that ratio is about one to twenty or five to seven percent. If we could double this percentage before the next generation matures, a different world would lie before us. The main purpose of writing this book is to show how seeking wisdom can change our lives and our communities. It is the writer's hope that someday these meek paragraphs can encourage others to seek wisdom and experience the exciting and rewarding lifestyle of the wise.

Contrast this with those who are never satisfied with anything. They always have something to complain about and look for someone to hear their complaints. They don't like what they have and are sure if they had more and better things, happiness would be in their corner. Not so; no matter what changes these complainers make, it will only fuel their fretting for more. Maybe what they have does not serve them well and maybe it's not the best, but there is a reason. What they have or don't have, they secretly curse (not necessarily through profanity), and what they curse will not bless them. Cursing life and what comes our way never leads to contentment. These are the same people who it is said can "hide today's sun with yesterday's clouds."

In contrast, observe the ways of the wise. They fret not about the things they cannot change nor do they fret about the things they can change, but rather set about to make the change. They also know how to bless their experiences and possessions rather than curse them. They know what is blessed will bless them. It is like a farmer who owned an old tractor. He would like to have had a new, larger tractor, but the one he had served him well and was dependable. Thus, he felt fortunate to be blessed and was grateful for what he had. He never felt the need to complain about the old tractor and lived with it until it outlived its usefulness. Unlike those who worship at the altar of materialism, the farmer was content.

Contentment is not passive nor is it blissful ignorance; it is the ripening of the spirit, mind and body together. Contentment is learning to live with the questions that can never be answered. It is living with the assurance that when answers to life's problems are needed, they will be handed to those who maintain an attitude of humility, show awareness and have courage.

The most calming benefit of contentment is knowing your decisions were based on the best information available to you the time. Knowing that you did not intentionally do anything wrong carries no guilt. If time proves you were wrong, it is knowing the past cannot be corrected. Trying to correct the past is like mixing a cake by stirring its contents in a clockwise motion. Once you realize an error has been made in adding its ingredients together, reversing your action to a counterclockwise motion will not "unmix" or return the ingredients to their natural state. This principle applies for those who experience losses in business, bad childhoods and failed marriages. The wise know you may have opportunities to make amends for past mistakes, but you must be content with not trying to fix the past; it's too late.

The strong, calm man is always loved and revered.
He is like a shade-giving tree in a thirsty land, or a
sheltering rock in a storm.
> —*As a Man Thinketh,* James Allen, p. 70

Chapter Three
Profiles in Wisdom

I owe gratitude to a multitude of people who were examples to me during my earlier years and especially those who came to me from wisdom. I recall six different individuals who literally changed my life and gave me new direction. It was only years later that the value of their influence was appreciated. These six individuals, as I would learn later, shared the same values and ideals one only finds in wisdom. Of course my family was always there to give me support for which I am grateful, but at this writing I am highlighting those individuals who ultimately were not responsible for my well being yet gave of themselves freely.

My second grade teacher was the first one outside of the family to encourage me when my troubles at school surfaced. At that time, a lot was going on in my family. My mother was in and out of the hospital several times that year with a heart condition, and my six-year-old brother was in recovery from a lung surgery.

I could not concentrate on schoolwork and experienced poor progress brought on by numerous mistakes with an "I don't care" attitude. Needless to say, I required more of the teacher's time and was at the bottom of the class in performance. Soon I had enough and left the room crying one day. I made it no further than the hallway outside the classroom and sat on the floor. To my surprise, my teacher, Mrs. Atkins, came out and sat down on the floor beside me, and with her arms around me we both cried. She promised me that if I were willing to work with her, she would help me become the kind of student who would always enjoy learning and would look forward to school. I agreed, and at that moment, the sympathy stopped and we returned to the classroom, where the challenge began.

I tell this story not because I was so touched by her sympathy, but because she, from wisdom, showed compassion. For the wise compassion does not mean just holding hands and crying together, but challenging you to overcome and be a better person. Mrs. Atkins and the other five people I look to as examples of wisdom refused to let me remain a victim. They would often make me wish I had never accepted their challenges, and they made me face the truth about myself, which was often painful. There were times I would try avoid at all costs seeing these people, knowing that I was falling short of the goals they encouraged me to follow. As I began to make progress, this changed and I began to be comfortable with these people and sought their company.

As for my second grade teacher, the story didn't end with the completion of second grade. In her declining years long after she retired, Mrs. Atkins was busy encouraging young teachers and helping others in developing their teaching skills. Once, she gave a lecture to a group of educators where she shared a story about a young boy in her class who experienced a series of crises and was having trouble with his studies. She told the educators how she challenged the student after spotting and understanding his despair. She then urged the teachers to be more aware of the conditions that often hinder learning. I was told her story ended successfully when she expressed satisfaction as to the progress made by this young man. Another one of my grade school teachers was present for the lecture and recognized the story was about me. Mrs. Atkins did not use a name in her lecture, but she did confirm with the other teacher that the story was indeed about me. Years later while I was in college, I saw Mrs. Atkins for the last time. She was on her hospital bed, which she never left, and was already blind. I'm sorry she could not see how I changed over the years, but I did make her aware of the changes I made because of her influence.

The other five individuals who influenced and guided me from their wisdom, I will not name, but will collectively discuss their contributions to me. Two of them were reasonably wealthy, but lived modestly, with humility, remembering their days of struggle. Three were in professions where generating wealth was not a consideration for success; one being a Methodist minister, one a school principal and the other a college professor. Of the remaining two, one was vice president of a large corporation, and the other a banker. Each of these, like Mrs. Atkins, applied what today's pop culture would call "tough love," but went far beyond that concept.

I was given constructive criticism that was often hard to take and sometimes hurt. The vice president, my immediate supervisor in employment, never allowed me to make a decision based on my own feelings, but forced me to look at all sides of a problem before acting. Thus, I learned to make objective decisions based on the overall good of the corporation and its clients. This was certainly a lesson in humility and awareness and saved me many embarrassing moments presenting cases in the boardroom. It was not easy nor was it fun to write and rewrite reports that would finally reflect clarity of purpose in every word and paragraph, but I would not trade anything for that experience.

One of these giants in wisdom spent many of his spare hours teaching me the art of public speaking; no, it wasn't one of the educators. He made sure I would not settle for being an average communicator, but a polished speaker capable of gaining and holding the attention of even the most sophisticated audience. The drilling was so intense at times I would get angry and vow not to go further with public speaking. I was in high school at the time and was engaged in public speaking contests with other schools and clubs. He encouraged me to consciously lose the accent that was trying to creep into my pattern of speech. I was not allowed to use contractions, but to pronounce each word precisely with proper inflections in each thought. The training was discouraging me until something strange started happening—I started winning contests. This training has opened doors for me over the years I would have never dreamed possible.

My involvement with this person did not stop with my learning public speaking, but went on to other social skills as well. We talked about all phases of etiquette including how to meet people, start casual conversations, proper dress codes for various occasions and other things my mother could have taught me if I would only have listened to her. This man had been places and done things that got the attention of most teenage boys. He was humble, admired by others and had all the qualities of a wise man. Today I am truly blessed to have had this person in my life.

The six people mentioned here are not the only people I found to have mastered the ideals of wisdom, but they are also the ones who influenced me most. Of the six mentioned, three were more intimately involved with my life than the other three but they all left a lasting influence on me. They made me aware there are higher and more exciting levels of living than the average person is willing to try. They lived life to the fullest, reached depths of understanding most people only read about, kept a cheerful attitude and were not boring. They all could share examples of hardships they experienced in their quest for wisdom. "Quest for wisdom" are my words, for these humble people would never admit they were wise. Their hardships were not just minor setbacks, but often major losses of family fortune and/or health. These are the types of losses that can violently shake and destroy the souls of the average sojourner. These men and women were often victims of tragedy, but refused to remain victims. They knew there were questions they could never answer, and they wasted no time arguing about them. Instead, they learned to live with the questions.

Following are some of the basic truths I learned from these role models:

1) Staying invested in our own victimhood prevents us from making changes.

2) Regardless of our circumstance in life, there are more opportunities at our doorstep than we can take advantage of in this lifetime.

3) The wise are never too busy or important to inspire and guide others.

4) The road to wisdom is paved with patience and persistence. There are no quick fixes or shortcuts.

5) The choices we make today create the reality we experience tomorrow.

Chapter Four
Substitutes for Wisdom

Left unattended, a vacant lot will continue to produce weeds and other unwanted plants. If properly cultivated, that same lot will produce meaningful and productive plants. Like the vacant lot, our minds left untended will find substitutes for meaningful thoughts and codes of behavior (*As a Man Thinketh*, James Allen, p. 11). For the majority of people who will never seek or understand wisdom, there are substitutes that always fall short of true wisdom. Since the mind cannot be without thought, standards of behavior based on wisdom must be consciously established to discourage substitutes. The most common substitutes are: common sense, conservatism/liberalism, political correctness, intelligence, education and knowledge. Common sense, intelligence, education and knowledge are all positive attributes; but they become negatives when they try to replace wisdom. The wise can deal with each of these without letting either control their behavior or overall beliefs. The only true standard for the wise is wisdom itself. They do not place labels on themselves such as conservative, liberal, or fundamental and do not follow the dictates of any particular discipline. Awareness, being one of the jewels in the crown of wisdom, allows the wise to recognize and avoid the substitutes and pitfalls used by others. Pitfalls are always part of any illusional concept. These concepts don't always measure up to truth and are not eternal. However, there are positives in some substitutes for wisdom. A good example of this is common sense.

Common Sense

Common sense may keep you out of trouble and prevent you from doing extremely foolish things, but it will never elevate you to a higher level. Relying on common sense is like always playing on the fifty-yard line. You will never lose yardage and will never move towards the goal line relying on common sense alone. Common sense comes from learning what is acceptable and reasonable in society and can, therefore, be taught. These lessons can prevent you from not fitting into what some others view as reasonable expectations. It is an example of how we start the process of teaching children the basic principles of acceptable behavior. Once learned, these can and should act as a springboard for seeking wisdom. Remember, wisdom itself cannot be taught or learned from others; it only comes from God (or universe, if you prefer).

A word of warning: common sense and all other substitutes for wisdom are taught and learned on the human level and will always contain errors and inconsistencies. Wisdom, on the other hand, always enters the human experience error free. This does not mean those who are wise live error free lives. The wise make their own choices and often contaminate the wisdom they received by filtering it through their prejudices and erroneous beliefs. That's why it is so important for the wise to continue to monitor their egos and make sure humility, the first jewel in the crown of wisdom, remains strong. Humility will keep you open-minded and prevent you from falling for substitutes, which on the surface may look attractive.

Conservatism and Liberalism

Conservatism and liberalism are just different sides of the same coin. Suppose the two sides of a nickel (heads and tails) began to argue with each other about which was the true representative of the coin and which provided the most value. One side may represent a liberal point of view and the other side a conservative one. Although their approach and point of view are different, they must each remember that together they are only worth five cents. With the absence of either the head or tails, the coin of political discourse would be worthless. Conservatism and liberalism are only in conflict with each other in the absence of the wisdom they replace.

Conservatives hold to the philosophy that there are values and concepts that always work and should be preserved. In the conservative movement you must be sure that ideas cherished are without error and are flexible. Those who hold to the liberal view of philosophy are usually unable or unwilling to distinguish between fundamentalism and conservatism. Fundamentalists usually side with conservatives against liberals, but they are vastly different in how far they go to preserve their beliefs. The average conservative is more tolerant than the fundamentalist, who rejects all attempts of science and modern concepts to shape society. In matters of religion, conservatives are often split on views regarding, for example, creation and evolution; but so are some liberals. Not so with ultra-liberals and fundamentalists. Ultra-liberals overwhelmingly believe in the evolution theory whereas fundamentalists never give up their belief in the literal story of creation. The wise refuse to enter this debate even though they have different views among themselves. The wise know how to live with questions for which there are no ready answers. This is just one example of issues that divide philosophies.

Political Correctness

Political correctness, another substitute for wisdom, made its appearance into liberal thinking during the 1960s. The movement was supposed to raise the sensitivity and awareness level of those who had previously accepted racism, sexism and suppression of the less fortunate as status quo behavior. What the political correctness movement has failed to recognize are the inconsistencies it created. For example, in their zeal to eliminate racism and sexism, multitudes of champions for these causes have crossed the line and they themselves have become racist and sexist. Once the line is crossed, the participants ignore tolerance by accepting as their role and privilege a self-righteous attitude. Because their original intent was noble, they feel the means chosen to achieve their goals should not be questioned. Too often the unspoken code of "I will love who you love if you will hate who I hate" pilots the politically correct mentality.

The wise have the same goals as the political correctness group, but their keen sense of awareness and humility prevents them from crossing the line. The desire for fairness by the politically correct led lawmakers to adopt a policy of trying to level the "playing field" for those who were previously disadvantaged, primarily women and minorities. Thus, affirmative action became law. Wisdom recognizes the inconsistency of how a concept designed to be inclusive can also be exclusionary by way of discrimination. The wise know two opposing concepts cannot effectively co-exist. Wisdom is always fair and sensitive to the feelings and needs of others.

Intelligence

To understand how intelligence can be a substitute for wisdom, it is important to know the difference between the intellect and wisdom. As stated in the introduction, wisdom comes from God (or the universe) and is without error. Intelligence implies your ability to logically reason and process information. Since some people are more intelligent than others, it can be argued that it too is a gift from God, given at birth. Intelligence, unlike wisdom, does not set a standard of conduct. Wisdom instills its own standards and is always noble.

Intelligence can and often does create its own errors and can become your own God. A high intellect (IQ) does not always assure success, nor does it assure noble decisions will be its result. Remember one of the jewels in the crown of wisdom is humility. This prevents the wise from ever using wisdom as a "snob factor." The universe will never give one a pure and noble gift to be used in a snobby way. There is no such thing as a wisdom snob. Intellectual snobs are quite common. No one is implying that a high IQ is not a noble gift, but it can be self-centered and self serving. Most of us know at least a few highly intelligent people who have difficulty interacting with others and functioning in a reasonable manner. Thus, they prevent themselves from making the world a better place by misusing their talents. It is the wise whose council and advice are always in demand. The ideal use of a high intelligence would be to seek wisdom. If intelligent men and women would use their gift of intellect to gain wisdom, they could make the world a better place for everyone. What an unbeatable combination!

Education

In his book, *The Status Seekers* (p. 24-38), Vance Packard refers to college graduates as the "diploma elite." Industry further promotes the elitism of education by rewarding those who hold a bachelor's degree or higher. The awards by private and public sectors not only extend to those with advanced degrees but to those who attended the so called elite universities and colleges. Unfortunately, academia does not have a monopoly on wisdom, nor are their graduates always more qualified to perform than those who do not hold degrees. In today's world of advanced technology, a degree often means that a person has achieved a proficiency level in a specified field of study but says nothing about their decision making or their level of wisdom. Today I stand in awe of those I find have achieved a high level of wisdom. Some have more education than I do and many of these people have less. It is a shame many of the highly educated members of society look down on others and use their education as a snob factor and as a substitute for wisdom.

Because of the high priority given to education in American society, it is assumed education is the only key to success. When you feel you haven't achieved the level of your desired success, it is natural to assume that it's lack of education. Seldom is it understood that it is not education, but social skills and wisdom that are lacking. Thus you seek more and more education, which may not be the answer. In cases of technical or specialized knowledge, it probably is. In its broader sense, education will never replace wisdom. It can, however, combine with wisdom (and sometimes intellect) to form an unbeatable force with wisdom leading the way.

Knowledge

Knowledge, like intellect and education, has a tendency to establish elitism. It demands status, higher incomes and privilege among those who possess technical or specialized knowledge. It can contain error, which can be passed on to others. An example of this is the Wright brothers' use of the French air tables, which contained errors. Before the Wright brothers could successfully fly their aircraft the errors had to be found and corrected.

Knowledge that is without error eliminates ignorance (especially cultural ignorance, which is the downfall of many politicians), promotes scientific endeavors and raises the quality of life. Unlike wisdom, knowledge can be passed on to others and accumulated. The printing press allowed knowledge to be accumulated and passed down from one generation to another in greater numbers than anyone ever dreamed possible. With all the benefits knowledge has to offer, it does not replace wisdom; but it can inspire us to seek wisdom, which is the sole purpose of this writing.

Chapter Five
The Wise Old Man and the Kites

The glory of young men is their strength; of old men, their experience.

—Proverbs 20:29 (RSV)

Experiences of the wise are the beacons for future generations. Wisdom cannot be taught, but experience, which can inspire us to seek wisdom, can be taught by instruction and example. Those who are wise hunger for opportunities to teach youth the basic essentials of life, especially those youth who face difficulties. The following story is an example of how the wise look for opportunities, find lessons in everyday scenarios and tactfully give instruction.

It had been a long winter, especially for Dan Morris, whose seventy-sixth birthday was only a few weeks away. It was his first winter alone since his wife of fifty-three years died in September of last year. Since that time, Dan (who the younger people referred to as the

"Old Man") spent his lonely days helping neighbors and friends with any odd jobs they needed done. Of course, they would pay him for his time, but his greatest reward was being with people who helped him cope with the loss of his wife. There had not been a lot to do in the way of outside chores during the cold days of winter, but now that spring was arriving, he was doing more walking around in the village. Dan enjoyed going down to the old general store to sit on its long bench outside and watch people he knew from the village pass by on their way to the city, which was about thirty-five miles away. He knew everyone who lived in the village and in most cases remembered their parents and kin. Over the years, both he and his wife had known all the ups and downs of almost all their neighbors. In fact, Dan knew things about his neighbors he would not dare repeat—things his neighbors would like him to forget.

While the usual rituals of spring were taking place throughout the village—such as spring vacation, spring cleaning, yard work and children playing—Dan was enjoying the warm sunshine on his favorite bench in front of the general store. The general store was now owned by a young fellow everyone called Gus, but it wasn't his real name. It was his grandfather's name, who owned and built the store years before his grandson was born. He had the store built of the finest logs and used the best craftsmen he could find. Log buildings were really on their way out and few people knew the trade.

As Dan soaked up the spring sun and reflected on times gone by, he was interrupted by the chatter of three excited young boys about the age of fourteen. The boys spoke politely to Dan as they approached, then entered the store as if they were in a hurry. Moments later they emerged with three new kites. Each spring the store always had kites on hand, going back to the time Gus' grandfather owned it. The boys immediately started assembling their kites on the opposite end of Dan's long bench, and he could tell this was the boys' first experience with kites.

After witnessing the way these boys were awkwardly going about their task, Dan spoke up and offered them assistance. In his most unassuming manner Dan asked, "Now you boys know you are going to have to put tails on those kites before they will fly?"

They looked somewhat puzzled before one of the boys spoke up. "You're kidding, aren't you? Besides, where would we find a tail for a kite?"

"Oh you have to make a tail for a kite, you can't go out and buy one," replied Dan. "I bet if you go back into the store, Gus can find you a box made of good stiff cardboard. Bring it out, and I will cut it up for you and show you how to make a tail for your kites." One of the boys soon came out with a small empty box that Dan skillfully cut into small sturdy rectangles and tied together. He showed the boys how to do it and made note that these tails would not work on any kite. Kite tails must be fitted to the size of the kites themselves.

The boys admitted they knew nothing about flying kites and that this was their first attempt at such. They thanked Dan (the "Old Man") and set out for Baker's Ridge in the rolling hills behind the general store, where there was always a steady breeze. At least they knew that much about flying kites, or maybe they were just copying what they saw others do in years gone by. As he watched the boys walk up the hill and out of sight, Dan remembered hearing rumors about these boys having behavior problems at school. Although he never had children of his own, Dan was always able to communicate with the youth of the village. Dan and his wife wasted no opportunity to welcome youngsters into their home. He was sure he remembered times when these boys' parents were guests in his home; maybe it was on those occasions when the youth of his church would be invited for homemade ice cream in his backyard. The friendships established during those times had been a lasting comfort, especially during the last few months after his wife's death. And, as was his nature, Dan somehow wished he could get to know these young fellows before it was too late.

Slightly more than an hour later, as he was getting ready to leave his bench to return home, Dan saw the boys returning from their kiting adventure. He waited to ask them how it went, hoping of course their venture had been a success. "Well boys, how did it go?" asked Dan as he noticed how badly damaged one of the kites appeared.

The boy carrying the damaged kite replied, "Not so good, my kite crashed to the ground when I let go the string." The second boy said he thought the wind was too strong and decided not to fly his kite today, but would save it for another day when the wind would be calmer. The other boy recounted his experience as being quite successful.

"Why did you let go of the string once the kite started flying?" inquired Dan to the boy holding the broken kite. "Well sir, we were trying to see which of us could make our kite fly highest and my string was running out. So, I thought if I let the string go, the kite would continue to climb, but instead it fell."

"So you thought the string was really holding the kite down, but wasn't it really holding it up?" asked Dan. After pondering the question for a few moments, the boys agreed with Dan's theory.

"You know," said Dan, "these lessons you fellows learned today remind me of the time when I was about your age. I thought the discipline and restrictions my parent and teachers put on me were like the kite string holding me back and preventing me from going higher in life. But actually they were holding me up, just as sure as the string was holding the kite up. Without these restrictions and guidelines, I would surely have failed. By holding to the strings, my parents and teachers allowed me to soar to heights that would have been impossible to reach on my own. They also allowed me to be pulled to safety and to soar even higher again and again.

"As for the kite that didn't fly because of the strong wind," continued Dan, "I, too, missed many adventures and opportunities waiting for my idea of perfect conditions. You know kites can't fly on calm days; there has to be some wind resistance before they can soar to any reasonable height. Learning to meet resistance now will strengthen your character. It will prepare you to handle future challenges. Besides, you boys would not want to fly with a pilot who only knew how to fly on clear and calm days. He would not be equipped for the challenges of flight.

"There are three things you fellows should never forget. First, never despise disciple or guidance; they keep you grounded, safe and will lift you to new heights. Secondly, don't wait for perfect conditions to act on your dreams and goals. All real successes involve risks. Finally, learn to master each adventure you encounter. Each time you fly your kite, it will become easier and more fun, as should all your other adventures and endeavors with regular practice." At this point, Dan had the full attention of each boy and they were sharing some of their adventures with him. He knew his message had not been too strong and that the boys were not turned off as though he were preaching to them. After all, fourteen-year-old boys don't take preaching very well.

Finally, Dan stood up from his bench and prepared to leave for home. He wished the boys good luck as they thanked him for helping with the kite tails. They walked with him a few blocks before turning off to their houses. Dan wondered if the boys would ever remember the lessons of the day. He would have been delighted to know that years later each of the boys, who were now men with children of their own, often reflected on the events of that day at the general store with the old man and the kites.

Chapter Six
Master or Slave

Becoming a victim is a tragedy; choosing to remain a victim is a self-imposed curse.

It was on the auction block where Mr. McDavid first met Jacob. Jacob, a slave in his thirties, was being sold by a plantation owner who was facing bankruptcy. The McDavid plantation needed more help to harvest the larger than usual cotton crop. The bidding started high for Jacob, and when it was finished he found himself shackled inside Mr. McDavid's wagon and on the way to his plantation.

As the harvest progressed, Jacob was proving a reliable and conscientious worker. The years went by; he was given more responsibility and was relied on to help oversee the activities of the other slaves. He worked well with the farm animals and, when they were sick or injured, he more often than the others knew what to do. In fact, he was often consulted about matters concerning harvesting, animal care, and the other slaves. Members of the McDavid household begin to rely more and more on Jacob's experience; after all, he had been working on plantations since he was thirteen.

One day as Jacob was working in the barn, one of the women slaves came to tell him that Mr. McDavid had passed away. Jacob knew at that moment his life would probably be different. Mrs. McDavid had died a few years before from pneumonia and Samuel Mc-David, their only heir, would now be in charge of the plantation. Jacob had watched young Samuel from the time he was about fourteen years old to his present age of thirty-five. Jacob himself was now in his late fifties and was concerned about Samuel's behavior with the animals and slaves. In fact, Samuel showed no respect for anyone or anything but himself.

Time proved Jacob right. Samuel became one of the most uncaring and ruthless plantation owners in the land. He spent most of his evenings gambling, drinking and partying. He would often come in past midnight on his horse and expect Jacob to be ready to take the horse to the stable for care and feeding. It was obvious that the horse had not been watered or fed all day while it was out. The horse would also show signs of having been beaten. Samuel would come into Jacob's quarters in a drunken state, get him out of bed and demand he come help him into the house before taking care of his horse. He did not hesitate to give Jacob a few whacks with his horsewhip during these episodes. The more money he lost on the night's gambling, the more ruthless he became. Despite the bad treatment at the hands of his master, Jacob remained loyal and steadfast.

It became evident in the community that Samuel McDavid was losing control of not only his plantation but also his life. No one trusted him anymore, and the young ladies of the community were beginning to fear and ignore him. His financial losses at the hands of experienced gamblers eventually forced him into bankruptcy. Realizing there was not enough money left to mend fences on the plantation or to buy the necessary seed to plant new crops or feed for his livestock, Samuel tried to borrow additional money for his already mortgaged plantation, but to no avail. Years before, bankers had labeled Samuel a poor risk. Seeing no way out, Samuel took his own life. The neighbors commented on what a waste his life had been. Here was a young man who had everything handed to him and gave it all away to his uncontrolled passions.

Jacob passed away a few years later, just before slavery was abolished. Everyone said it was a shame that he could not have lived long enough to experience freedom. True, Jacob never became free in a physical sense, but he was free in mind and spirit to respond to his circumstance. In saying this, I am not trying to trivialize the plight of plantation slaves, which in themselves were a tragedy. To understand this concept, you need to know all plantation slaves were not alike. They were a heterogeneous group in how they reacted to their circumstance, in their variety of skills and their levels of proficiency.

Compare Jacob's life with that of Samuel, who died a despised and feared man. At first glance, one would think this was a tragic tale about master and slave; Samuel being the master and Jacob the slave. Looking at this story through the eyes of wisdom you would be forced to examine which man was slave and which one was master. Jacob, a man bought and owned by another, was not only slave but also master of his passions and temperaments. He learned from adversity and stayed in control, accepting that which he could not change and changing that which was within his own power. Thus, he became a trusted servant making a difference in the lives of his fellow slaves. He also chose to be a good steward in the care taking of the plantation's assets. He could have been defiant but chose to remain in control of his own passions as any wise man would do. Throughout his ordeal as slave, Jacob wore the crown of wisdom with its four jewels of humility, awareness, courage and contentment.

Samuel, unlike Jacob, played the role of master but was slave to his own passions, desires and habits. He surrendered his life to gambling, alcohol and reckless spending. He ignored responsibility, was not a good steward of his holdings and had no regard for the feelings of others. In fact, in today's society he would be classified as a sociopath, one who uses people as objects for his own purpose. His abuse of others prevented him from ever knowing humility, which is the first step in becoming wise. Samuel showed no awareness in realizing the results of his careless and reckless habits nor did he have the courage to change. He followed his passions like a sheep being led to slaughter, and they destroyed him. Thus he remained a slave to them unto the end and never knew the rewards of contentment. He volunteered to become a slave whereas Jacob became a slave not of his own choosing. Even in bondage, Jacob enjoyed many of the freedoms that were denied Samuel, who sold out his freedoms to his passions, only because he refused to learn from consequences sent his way.

The man who reins in his passions will never have to wear their yoke.

Chapter Seven
Creating Dragons

Fear can be real, but it is often the dragon we create to avoid facing responsibility.

Standards of decision making by the wise differ greatly from those of others. The wise make their decisions without the baggage of prejudice, hate, fear or superstition. Often, others make decisions not based on facts are but how facts are interpreted. The natural tendency is to filter facts and truth through our egos, background and experiences. If we have been taught a particular discipline, you can bet our decisions will reflect that teaching. Not so with the wise, who, through their humility and awareness, are able to discount factors that cloud logic. The end result is they have a reason for the decisions they make. These reasons always involve evidences of responsibility and never fall to the level of excuses. The wise and responsible people have reasons for their action or inaction; others have excuses.

Reasons are usually directed towards a particular situation at a particular time, whereas excuses often deal with ongoing behavior. For example: a teacher might ask a student, "Why were you late today?" The student may reply he was late because the road was closed. This answer is a reason involving a temporary problem. It shows the student took responsibility to select an alternate route and thus completed his journey. Excuses, on the other hand, show no elements of responsibility and usually involve situations that may not be temporary. Examples of this are when a teacher asks a student why he did not attend school yesterday. His reply may also be because the road was closed. This is an excuse, not a reason, and shows no responsibility in his trying to arrive at school. The teacher could have easily asked, "Why are you always late?" Even the question itself implies a long-term problem. The student may reply he is always late because he oversleeps, thus, an example of not being responsible. A reason can also become an appropriate response to a long-term situation. When this happens, reason moves into another category; it then becomes an "obvious reason." For example, someone may ask the question, "Why don't you ride the subway to work?" The reply may be, "There are no subways in our city," an example of an obvious reason.

There are always reasons for behavior, and they are

part of the decision making process. Excuses are not involved with responsible decision making and should be eliminated at all costs. They are excess baggage that the foolish insist on preserving. They are the building blocks for failure. Failure that is temporary requires no excuses and provides a learning experience, but failure with excuses gives you no incentive to improve. The mind can construct any scenario, real or not, based on the excess baggage it has collected over the years. When imaginary scenarios are acted upon, excuses around it grow and become more elaborate. They give you a false sense of reality. Reality never needs excuses, only reasons. It has been noted that losers have more excuses than winners.

Fostering an abundance of excuses eventually leads you to create an exaggerated, unreal view of life. Thus, you begin to imagine things as being bigger, more dangerous and more threatening than they really are. Fear that was never a factor until now suddenly enters the picture. This process is referred to as creating dragons. Legendary dragons exist not in reality but in the minds of man. They can be as big as you want, or they can be destroyed with logic and reason. Once the dragon is destroyed, its reason for being created may still exist, but in a more manageable size. Examples of dragons are: racism, sexism, poverty, heredity, lack of education and lack of opportunities. In reality, racism exists; but making a dragon of it can lead you to cross the line and become a racist yourself, ignoring the fact that more opportunities are available than anyone can use in their lifetime. The same is true with sexism: you can become a sexist trying to prevent it. Other dragons can paralyze you from taking action, but once the dragon is slain, the problem becomes smaller and can be eliminated. An example of this is when we label bad habits as addictions. Addictions are the dragons that we give control over us. When dragons are created, the creators try to make us believe they are real. This relieves them of taking responsibility, gives them victim status and allows them to adopt unrealistic behavior without being questioned. The following story is an excellent example how this plays out.

Once, long ago in a small kingdom, there lived a successful landowner who was quite wealthy. His wealth came from having bred some of the best cattle in the area and growing the finest crops. He had two sons who were approaching the ages where they would be called on to help around the estate, thus allowing their aging father more free time. It would also save his having to hire outside help.

One morning when the father went out to inspect his fields, he found something had destroyed some of his crops that were already scheduled for harvest. Further investigation also revealed that at least two of his youngest calves had been killed and partially eaten. He asked his sons to go into the forest to look for a possible predator that might be responsible for this deed. For several days the two boys looked, but found nothing.

Now in those days, people believed in dragons, but no one had ever actually seen a dragon. So the boys decided the culprit must be one of those illusive dragons. This was the story they brought back to their to father, who had no reason to doubt them because in the back of his mind he thought there just might be dragons living in the forest. A few days later, the boys found some large green lizards and several large eggs of unknown origin. When they returned to the estate, they proceeded to convince their father the eggs were from dragons and the lizards were hatched from the eggs of the same type. This was their proof for existence of dragons.

Their argument was so convincing they had their father agree the boys needed more armed men to help them hunt dragons. Men hired to tend the cattle and crops were taken from their regular tasks to now hunt dragons. Funds set aside to plant and harvest crops and feed the cattle were converted to swords, shields and other armor. The hunt for dragons went on for months and eventually years. The boys were still convincing their family they needed more funds to properly protect the estate when in reality all they were doing was playing soldiers at the expense of their family.

Before long it became evident the estate was spending more than its current income. The father was getting feebler by the day and had long since been unable to work, but he still believed in his sons. Eventually the father passed away and the sons inherited the estate.

Not realizing the foolishness of their actions over the last few years, they were astonished to discover the large amount of debt they were now facing. With no skills, no money to cover debts and no funds to hire workers, the brothers were forced to relinquish the estate over to its creditors.

This is a story of two young men who had everything laid out before them and squandered it all because they found it easier to create dragons rather than take advantage of the opportunities available. The wise know creating dragons paralyzes you from seeing opportunities and making wise choices. When discrimination, racism, sexism and cruelty confront us, we have a choice of either going around them to look for opportunities or using them to create dragons. Since dragons are created in the mind of man, there is no limit to how large they can become.

Our dragons are only as large as we choose to make them.

Chapter Eight
Wisdom and Religion

Who can separate his faith from his actions, or his belief from his occupations?
—The Prophet, Kahlil Gibran, p. 84

To understand religion, you must reinforce the conviction that body, mind and soul comprise the total sum of one's being. Any emphasis on either of these three affects and may alter the total character of the individual. Thus religion cannot be separated from choices and actions. The wise are sojourners and believe their goal is to absorb all that life has to offer and learn from it. They are acutely aware that their choices in work, play and rest will reveal their inner beliefs and thoughts.

Take the example of Jim, who had been a counselor at a youth camp for more than two decades and was contemplating retirement. One day in early summer, he was approached by the camp manager, who asked if he would be willing to be in charge of a group of inner-city boys who had problems at school and with the police. Jim had never worked with these problems before since the campers in the past had come from stable and successful families. He reluctantly accepted the challenge, but immediately began to wonder if he had done the right thing.

The day before the campers were to arrive, Jim walked to the lake on the north side of the camp to watch the sunset. As he strolled along, he picked up a handful of small stones and began throwing them into the lake and skipping them across the surface of the water. He noticed how quickly they disappeared out of sight when their motion stopped. Jim wondered how it might feel to be that stone which once on the bottom would never go anywhere unless someone or something moved it. He thought how the outside of the stone would always be surrounded by water, but the inside would always be dry due to its tightly packed composition. The stone would never enjoy the cool refreshing water of the lake on its inside.

Suddenly Jim noticed an object floating on the surface of the lake and being carried by the ripples in the water. As the object moved closer to him, he was able to identify it as a sponge. He thought what it must be like to be a sponge floating on top of the water while the stone lay on the bottom doing nothing. By that time the sun was down, and Jim knew he had better go home and prepare himself for the arrival of his new campers. They were scheduled to arrive that night and would be in his care by early noon tomorrow.

The next day Jim arrived a camp and met the group of boys who would be in his charge for the next week. The boys had already begun to complain and made up their minds the week would be a waste of time. After several minutes of trying to get their attention, Jim went to his car and pulled out a bag containing a large item. He then invited the boys to follow him down to the lake. Once at the lake he reached into his bag and removed a large commercial sponge, purchased the night before, and threw it into the water. The sponge started moving, propelled by the wind and the ripples the wind created. He then reached down and picked up five smooth stones that he threw into the water one by one. By this time he had the attention of each boy in the group.

"Okay," said Jim, "while you are here this week, I want each of you to remember this demonstration and what it represents. Notice what happened to the stones and what is now happening to the sponge. The sponge is experiencing all that the lake has to offer. There is not a molecule of water in the lake off limits to the sponge. Water can flow through the sponge, and the sponge can flow through the water unrestricted. The stones, on the other hand, are hardened and closed. They can never experience the fullness of the lake because they can't flow through its waters and cannot experience having its waters flow through them. Which would you rather be, the sponge or the stone? While you are here this week, if you are to get anything from your experience, you must behave like the sponge. Your other choice is to become cold, hard and rigid. If you choose this option, you will experience nothing. This lesson does not end when you leave this camp; it will follow you for the rest of your life. The decisions you make today will have to be made over and over for the rest of your life. They will cover your beliefs, your thoughts and your actions. They will be your religion."

In understanding the true meaning of religion, the wise know it is at the core of their own being and is not the same as organized religion. Religion is to organized religion as education is to school. Education is the end product of two different school functions; one being to educate, which is the process of systematically providing instruction and discipline. The other is to educe, the process of bringing out that which is latent, hidden or reserved within an individual (*Webster's New Collegiate Dictionary*, 2nd Edition, 1956). The purpose of organized religion is the same as that of the school, but with emphasis on spiritual development. Unfor-

tunately, organized religions are perhaps the most frag-
mented institutions in the world. There is not one of
the five major organized religions where there is unanimous or near unanimous agreement on any philo-
sophical discipline. Thus, the organization commonly
referred to as the church, mosque, synagogue, temple
or shrine is not your religion any more than the term
"school" is your education.

The problem with organized religion is that many
of its disciplines are based on man's interpretation of
spiritual principles, which can often be in error and
have little or nothing to do with spiritual matters. In
many cases, this leads to the establishment of elite sects,
denominations or cults. Examples of elitism are when
those adhering to a particular belief feel their belief is
the only true one and everything else is wrong. Those
outside of organized religion view this trend negatively
and want nothing to do with it. Unfortunately, they
never learn the difference between religion and the
institutions of organized religion.

The U.S. Army, in the past, provided a manual for
the spouses of military officers, advising them to wear
their husband or wife's rank in their hearts and not on
their shoulders. Creating elitism in religion is only an
act of wearing your faith on your shoulders for others
to see and has nothing to do spiritual growth. The wise
are clear on this point and do not get involved with

playing the game of elitism. The wise do, however, often disagree with each other on matters of the spirit, but due to their respect for the others' wisdom, they don't attack or feel superior.

Spiritual leaders have an awesome responsibility in leading followers of the faith to spiritual awareness. It is in this context that a heightened sense of awareness by the minister, rabbi, priest, guru, etc. is required to prevent sending confusing signals. Without awareness these leaders can quickly lose the confidence and support of followers by subconsciously adopting lifestyles contradictory to their teachings. The signal sent then implies a life that is out of control. Followers question how someone who is out of control can help them live a controlled life free from excesses. Failure to be aware of these pitfalls brings out the scoffers against organized religion. It is interesting, however, that most scoffers of organized religion are avid supporters of public education even when it fails.

Chapter Nine
Wisdom and the Three Fs:
Fortune, Fame and Fashion

Suppose someone made the statement to you that they were born in a poor, upper-class family. What would your reaction be? The overwhelming majority of those in western cultures would conclude the term "poor, upper-class family" as contradictory or an oxymoron. Western world culture assumes that admission to the upper class requires wealth. To a lesser degree, it is expected that members of the upper class achieve fame at some level and have a flair for fashion. The wise have their own standards for achieving upper-class status by knowing that fame, fortune and fashion are temporary, fleeting and illusional. The real upper class is only available to those whose standards are eternal, standards such as virtue, truth, justice, humility and courage. These attributes are grounded in wisdom. In his song lyrics, "Don't Cry for Me Argentina," from the Broadway production of *Evita*, Tim Rice further reminds us that goals of just fame and fortune are not real but are illusions and not solutions.

The wise are quick to recognize what is real and refuse to chase illusions. They never consider themselves better or worse than anyone else and refuse to make the comparison. They do not compete with others for status, but daily compete with their former selves, relying on wisdom to light their pathway. They are not class conscious and do not depend on others for approval. They are admired by all people from all stations of life, but will never admit to their place in the "real upper class." The wise often experience conflict when others insist on pursuing goals that are not real. These are often the people who are quick to label the wise as arrogant when ideas conflict. Since these people follow illusional standards, they fail to understand the "firmness of mind" enjoyed by the wise and confuse it with arrogance. The unwise or the foolish are the ones who themselves practice arrogance by supporting unreal standards which are as temporary as bubbles in a boiling pot.

Fortune

The man who has no money is poor, he who has nothing but money is poorer still.

—Anonymous

Regarding wealth, it is impossible to set a goal of just becoming wealthy. True wealth is not a goal itself, but rather the result of goals that are noble. Noble goals can be gauged, measured and focused. An example is an architect who is determined to learn all he can about his profession by studying the most advanced concepts in his field and experimenting with new ideas to improve those concepts. As the quality of his services improve, so will the demand for his services. Also, the appropriate level of income will follow and go far beyond that of any other architect whose only goal was to produce wealth. The laws of compensation act within the framework of noble goals on the premise that income levels are dependent on: 1) the complexity of the job to be done; 2) the number of skilled people available to handle the task; and 3) the level of skill each worker may possess. The possession of wealth is a real blessing if based on these ideals, but wealth ill-gotten can be a curse. Ill-gotten wealth will always, sooner or later, possess and destroy the wealthy.

Without noble goals, the mind will fill the gap (left by the absence of logical thought) with ideas that may not be honorable. For example, the desire to acquire wealth tempts you to adopt unfair practices of cheating, stealing, deceiving and lying. To further understand noble goals, take the example of the student who has set her goal to only get good grades. This would be an illusional goal and can be reached by noble and dishonest methods. A noble goal of trying to learn all you can in each subject will not only produce good grades, but also will instill proficiency and build character. It will eliminate the temptation for cheating on tests, plagiarizing and grade changing. Shallow and illusional dreams must be covered by noble goals that are always error free. Sure, good grades lead to better employment opportunities, admission to advance studies and prestige in the academic community, but without noble goals of proficiency, the student will not rise to the standards enjoyed by the wise.

The bottom line in understanding wealth is that desiring it without a noble goal is not in itself noble and will never become the panacea you seek. Unfortunately, inherited wealth is seldom appreciated as much as for those who earn it. Those who earn wealth by noble means are humbled by their own accomplishments, remembering the struggles and sacrifices they endured.

Creation of wealth is essential to a stable economy, but it is not a requirement for all citizens to be wealthy. Some professionals such as clergy or public school teachers know from the outset they are not in careers that require production of wealth. Stockbrokers, business owners, investment counselors, investors and industrialists must develop a talent for generating wealth by honorable means. In a capitalistic society, wealth created finds its way into the economy for jobs to produce goods and services. These goods and services add to the quality of life for all citizens. Investments made by the very wealthy create grants to needy students to pursue studies at colleges and universities. Wealth invested in utility companies help keep the cost of services down.

Without these investments, some people could not afford the enormous cost of utilities. Wealth also provides public funds for municipal services through taxes and bonds. It's interesting how many people in a capitalistic society despise even those who produce wealth by honorable means. Often the scoffers of the wealthy are the very students who are in schools that were created and/or funded by the wealthy. Scoffers are often those who are also receiving grants or scholarships made possible by the wealthy. The same is true for workers whose jobs were made possible by someone's talent for producing riches. True, wealth can and is often misused. The greatest misuse of wealth is to hoard it. The most honorable use of wealth is to invest it in worthwhile endeavors. Let your wealth work for you and others.

Fame

The standards and procedures discussed herein

have so far been applied to the subject of wealth, but they also apply to the subject of fame. Fame is fragile and fleeting if it is not based on the ideals of wisdom and acquired by real or noble goals. Like fortune, fame can be a real blessing, but can also be a curse. It is not a one-way ticket to the real upper class unless it is based on standards, which are eternal. The mere hungering for fame can lead you into undesirable territories for which you may not be prepared. When this happens, a number of options present themselves for saving the fleeting illusion of fame. These options are not always noble, but are used in desperation to fan the waning flames of the illusion. Options to be avoided at all costs are bribery, deception, arrogance and vanity.

The most desirable and lasting characteristic a famous person can possess is humility, which is one of the jewels of wisdom. Fame only lasts as long as the famous can attract others; but in the absence of humility, this may not be possible. Fame as a true and lasting virtue carries with it an awesome responsibility. Whether the famous like it or not, someone will always look to them as a role model. Thus, they carry the burden of trying to be a positive example. Depending on their level of fame, any misguided goals or illusions will be revealed to the world and will damage, impair or impede their future success. Two excellent examples of this are Napoleon and Hitler, who achieved fame under false pretenses and later allowed their true selves to be revealed, only to be despised and hated. Compare these with famous people like Abraham Lincoln and Mother Teresa, whose steadfast examples were laced with wisdom and virtue.

Fashion

Few disciplines in life control and enslave the thoughts and actions of people more than fashion. Fashion robs self-worth, squanders wealth to keep abreast of trends, challenges health and often becomes a false god for many. To worship the god of fashion, you are asked to blindly follow the rules of the trendsetters no matter how ridiculous they may be. Once these trends are accepted, income and resources are taken away from the family treasury for sacrifices on the altar of the fashion gods.

The reasonable people of any day and in any period of time use fashion tastefully and within the framework of modesty. Many career opportunities have been missed because of improper dress or excessive attention given to trendy fashions.

The foolish in any society can be found following the most ridiculous fads and trends just to be in vogue with their idols. Teenagers may often create a financial burden for their families by trying to keep in style, but so can an irresponsible adult. Thus the statement,

"Fashion taxes without reason and collects without mercy," proves to be true.

The wise are not trendy nor do they allow fashion to dictate behavior. They are always aware of what is reasonable and tasteful. They never feel the need to be seen with the right crowd although they may often be invited. If they are not invited, there is no fretting or feeling of being left out: they leave that up to the ones who must attend to maintain their status.

Chapter Ten
Wisdom, Sex, Marriage and Family

Sexual Energy and Expression

Probably the most difficult and controversial emotion to control and master is the natural desire for sexual expression. In his book, *Think and Grow Rich*, Napoleon Hill describes sexual energy as an asset (p. 175-196). Often, those with high sexual energy consider it a curse and allow it to control them instead of using it for positive achievement. This may seem like a contradictory idea, but to the wise it is not.

The wise often have high levels of sex energy and use them to their benefit. When sexual energy is properly channeled, it makes you more radiant, alive and enthusiastic. Thus, those people rise earlier, complain less and get more done overall. Napoleon Hill cites that others are attracted to them and can sense the magnetism they exude in their voice, their handshake, their smile and their touch (*Think and Grow Rich*, p. 187). They are neat and clean in appearance, but may not be the most beautiful people in the room. They will, however, be the ones people will be drawn to first. Their preference for sexual expression is having one partner, in marriage, with an equal appetite for intimacy. This is not to say there are not sometimes partners outside of marriage for both men and women, as Napoleon Hill reports, but is not the usual practice for the wise nor is it a lasting practice for those who understand the benefits of sexual energy.

For the foolish, a high sex energy is a curse that destroys confidence, ages the body and worships at the altar of instant gratification. Eventually they will experience disillusion, bitterness and loss. When your highest priority is instant gratification, futures are compromised, fortunes are compromised and poverty is assured. Some will argue that those who always seek instant sexual gratification at the risk of losing it all suffer from an addiction to sex. The wise know there is never an addiction to anything for which there is always a conscious choice. Each instant and each act is a choice of free will as long as you are not being forced. Giving in to an emotion for instant gratification is not the way of the wise and does not show courage. Of course, sex energy is used for the pleasure of enjoying sex, but a high level of sex energy goes beyond and into your other endeavors. Used wisely, it can be the fuel that propels you to greater achievements.

Marriage

Married life will not go by itself, or if it does it will not stay on track. It will turn off at every switch and fly off at every turn or impediment. It needs a couple of good conductors who understand the engineering of life.

—*Royal Path of Life,* T.L. Haines and L.W. Yaggy, p. 461

The wise know the purpose of marriage is to give stability to society. You have no trouble finding critics of this concept using examples of dysfunctional families. When families breakup or divorce, chaos reigns. Children of these homes react in one of two ways: they either rebel and develop a negative view of marriage, or they resolve to avoid the pitfalls of their parents. In choosing a partner for marriage, you should never marry hoping or thinking the other person will make you happy and satisfy your needs. You should choose someone with whom you can share your own happiness. Marriage reaches it highest potential when both partners marry to share the happiness they already possess. The wise never expect happiness to come from another, especially their marriage partner. To do so would give all the power for happiness to one partner. Failure on the part of that partner to bring happiness into the marriage will create bitterness and lead to chaos.

Before considering marriage, the wise ask themselves: "Is this the right person for me, am I the right person for her (him) and can I offer what it takes for a harmonious life together?" This is assuming, of course, these two are already in love but knowing love is not enough to build a solid union. When cohabitation seems to become more acceptable, the wise know it is not the same level of commitment as marriage. The marriage vow, the ultimate in relationships between mortals, is designed for stability, but it is not the only way stability is offered to society. Stability, without a doubt, is the cornerstone of contentment, one of wisdom's jewels.

Few marriages start and end in a "happily ever after" mode. Most marriages have problems and end in success only because each partner is committed to making the relationship work. These marriages are stronger than those with few or no major problems. In these marriages the couple learns through time and experience the joys of love, devotion and respect. Notice how a very elderly couple will still hold hands and smile at each other. Even if their sex life is no longer active and their physical beauty has suffered, they are held together as one by the inner beauty they both share. Don't try to convince these people that Romeo and Juliet was the greatest love story of the ages. They know better because they live it.

I wrote the following message for my daughter Rhonda and her husband Todd Blair on their wedding day. I had the privilege of reading these words during the wedding ceremony:

Today each of you are receiving your rings as a token of your love and commitment to each other. Your rings are now new, unsoiled and without cuts or scrapes. As time passes, they will lose some of their luster and will require some polishing, but so will your marriage. Your rings will also endure cuts and scrapes. If they are made of the right stuff (usually gold), cuts and scrapes will only reveal more gold. Likewise, your marriage, if made of the right stuff, will reflect more of its luster and strength as it experiences scrapes. Look at your rings often and remember they are symbols of your union together. When they seem to lose their luster, apply polish. Like your rings, your life together will require frequent polishing with love, respect and kindness. Do this often and consider your marriage as an enduring gift to each other, symbolized by your rings.

Mastering the art of decision making in marriage is one of the strongest traits of the wise. It unifies, establishes authority, designates responsibility and gives clarity to all parties involved in the outcome of any decision. Decision making in marriage is always the joint responsibility of husband and wife and should be made in the best and safest interest of the family. The final decision must represent a unified front before it is given to the other family members. Each of the other parties involved will either have a preference or a choice in its outcome. I call this the choice/preference ratio.

An example of the choice/preference ratio is when at birth a child has 0% choice in any decision, but has 100% preference. Parents then have 100% choice and 0% preference for decisions made on behalf of the child. As the child ages, the c/p ratio is reversed. The child will eventually have 100% choice, and the parent will have no choice in his child's decisions but will always have preferences (100%) as to the decisions the child makes. There is no magic age when the c/p ratio changes between parent and child; it all depends on the level of independence of the child. Parents who support a child through college age may have a ratio of 50% choice and 50% preference, same as the student. Another child at college age may be more self-supporting and have 80% choice ratio thus giving the parents more preferences and less choices in the child's decisions. Understanding this process gives harmony to family structures and assures smoother transitions from childhood to responsible adulthood. It also defines for parents guidelines for dealing with their now adult children and their spouses. It clarifies responsibilities and keeps people from trying to get involved in the affairs of others without cause.

In large, close families, there is a tendency to become intimately involved in each other's decisions and personal problems, which often causes conflict among its members. This process is known as enmeshment; from the word enmesh, which means "to entangle in or as in meshes" (*Webster's New Collegiate Dictionary*, 2nd Edition, 1956). Being enmeshed in the affairs of family always makes it more difficult to gain independence without causing controversy. It is especially stressful and difficult for someone marrying into a family where enmeshment is common.

The wise are always aware of who has responsibility for choices and tries to stay out of affairs of others. However, there may be times when suggestions are made to influence a choice, but unless there is a stake in the outcome, these suggestions are only preferences.

I had a young couple ask me recently what was the most important point to remember in raising children. My response was to never take away all their consequences. This practice would give children the impression they don't have to follow rules. In doing so, children are thus robbed of valuable learning experiences. It is not the role of the parent to always make their children happy, but to raise them to become responsible, productive citizens who can create their own happiness.

In raising child prodigies or gifted children, parents often walk a tightrope knowing their child's level of special gifts exceed his/her level of emotional maturity. There is a tendency to make the child feel special and give them privileges not afforded others. Without consequences the child may grow up to expect or even demand privileges without reason. If taken to extremes, sociopathic tendencies may be exhibited in adulthood.

Chapter Eleven
Wisdom and Politics

Personal power is always greater than political power and must always come first.

In any democracy or republic where citizens elect leaders, there will always be those who disagree with elected officials and those who will support them blindly. Those who support candidates that lose elections often carry their bitterness and disappointments with them until the next election only to be bitter again if their candidate or party loses. If their candidate wins, there is instant elation. The wise do not play this game but overcome its temptation knowing that personal power is always greater than political power. Millions of books and pages have been written about those who gained personal power in times and settings where governments failed by being oppressive or weak. In these times it was the wise that came to the rescue of the suffering citizens. These wise men and women are honored by history whereas the oppressors are scorned.

Voting in an election is a privilege that carries with it a great responsibility. Voters should evaluate each candidate based on their overall decision making history and never on their party affiliation or their "pie in the sky" promises. The wise vote for candidates based on how they follow the basic principles of wisdom, even at the risk of being unpopular. It is the voter's responsibility to evaluate each person vying for a public office and to avoid the trap of letting special interest groups influence their vote. You should recognize that some organizations always endorse certain political parties and will only give a biased opinion. In general elections, the wise never hesitate to vote a split ticket, giving their votes to more than one party. They have enough confidence in their decision making to choose wisely without following strict party lines. Voting in the United States is an exercise the framers of the Constitution assumed would be carried out by rational people making rational and sane decisions. It was further hoped that voters would most often have the best interest of the country in mind.

In deciding how to vote or which issue to support, the wise have three choices. They can support the liberal point of view, the conservative one or neither. The choice is like having two cloaks in the closet, one being liberal, and the other conservative. At any given time, only one cloak will be selected and worn, based on the political climate and circumstance at the time. The other one will remain in the closet for later use. There may be times when neither is appropriate and are both left in the closet. Those who practice partisan politics only have one cloak and wear it all time.

The wise will not say, "I will never vote for a Democrat (or Republican)," but will say only that voting for the candidate is more important than partisan politics. In being partisan, the voter must determine if the candidate is capable and willing to go outside the party platform to support issues more beneficial to the country than his or her own agenda. If the answer is no, it would be wrong to support that candidate. Unfortunately, the foolish candidate seeks office only to gain power, whereas the wise candidate seeks office to promote his or her feeling of responsibility towards a noble cause. Leaders who make sound decisions based on the ideals of wisdom bring out the best in citizens of the country. Leaders who support legislation allowing citizens to engage in weak and cowardly behavior will eventually bring out the worst in its citizens. Examples of this are state supported gambling (lottery), abortions, partial-birth abortions and increased dependency on government. State supported lotteries are often just a confession by the state that taxpayer money has been wasted, and they encourage citizens to gamble. This brings more money into government coffers, but at what cost to the moral character of its citizens? Governments claim the lottery brings more money for schools and services that benefit all people, but there is a strong argument to support the argument that sound fiscal policies of eliminating wasteful spending would be more effective. Gambling often instills in the minds of the very impressionable a "get something for nothing" attitude.

Another example of decisions gone bad is the subject of abortion. If abortion remains a medical or legal decision by responsible professionals, it has its place in a civilized society. If abortions are decided outside of medical and legal considerations, it is usually done for selfish reasons. Those selfish reasons are for personal convenience or to avoid a consequence. Avoiding consequences destroys character. Preventing consequences builds character. In the case of abortions, a consequence is prevented by preventing the unwanted pregnancy in the first place. If the pregnancy occurs and is not wanted, a noble decision would be to face the consequence and offer the child up for adoption. Too many candidates have either won or lost elections based only on their decisions about abortions. To elect candidates only on one issue is a misuse of the political process.

Another example of bad decisions by elected officials is to encourage voters to become more dependent on government. True, government has the responsibility of providing a safe environment for its citizens and an atmosphere of fair trade for each, but not to provide one's total needs cradle-to-grave. There are literally millions of voters who vote in every election but have never made a critical decision as to the candidates' stand on the issues. They simply wait to see how their favorite party or special interest group, which is in most cases a labor union, will vote. They further wait to receive preprinted handouts that resemble the legal ballots. They then take these into the voting booth and simply copy them onto the ballot itself. When they leave the polling place and discard the handouts, these voters can seldom tell you whom any of the local or candidates were. This is not voting, but just ballot marking to register someone else's decision. The voter's personal responsibility is thus relinquished and given over to special interests groups that promise to care for all needs. These examples are the result of people depending on government, handing their personal power over to elected officials and keeping a "something for nothing" attitude in politics.

Unfortunately, there are people who have never been a contributor to society but have always depended on government for everything. They entered the welfare system as a child and as teenagers gave birth out of wedlock to at least one child, but more often many more. As aging mothers with dependents, they rely on federal, state and/or county funds for their livelihood. Later they may find themselves caring for grandchildren as they themselves approach senior years and become eligible for yet another level of government benefit. There is no question that their vote will blindly go to the candidate who supports their victim status and promises more. This is not to single out mothers, but it is one example of dependency. Other examples of dependency are milking the unemployment fund by filing false reports about job seeking or filing false reports concerning disability benefits, all under the belief that the government is obligated to care for all our needs. These are games the wise do not play. The wise know there are unfortunate circumstances, medical or otherwise, which prevent some people from being able to be fully self-supporting; and in these cases assistance should be available. They also know others have abused the system for selfish personal gain.

If the wise wish to logically discuss politics, they do not confer with ultra-liberals or ultra-conservatives, who are by far the most boring and biased people on earth. Through their lack of awareness, they can never see but one point of view, and even then they do not see clearly. The real voters are the ones who can hear both sides of an issue and make decisions accordingly. It is the truly wise, however, that can listen to both sides of an issue and feel confident in making decisions that may not bring personal comfort but will bring the most good to the most people.

Chapter Twelve
Bread

A gnawing hunger for wisdom never goes unsatisfied.

Once there was a small kingdom ruled jointly by a benevolent King and Queen and located deep in the forests of Bavaria. They were blessed with a son who showed great promise and was designated to become heir to the throne. Early in his life, the young Prince developed a fascination with all kinds of foods and their preparation. With not much to do in the castle after his daily tutoring, he spent much of his free time with the chefs and cooks in preparing and tasting foods that came into the kingdom from all parts of the world. Soon all of his favorite foods lost their appeal no matter how many different ways they were prepared. More foods of different varieties were bought in and they too failed to satisfy.

After many years of not liking any of the foods of his youth, the Prince decided to set out on his own to try and find the best food in the whole world. He started out on foot early one morning at sunrise while the dew was still on the grass and while the fog was still clinging to forest floor. At about midmorning, he was beginning to tire when he heard a noise coming through the trees. As he approached the area where the noise was coming from, he encountered a woodcutter at work. Being somewhat startled, the woodcutter asked, "What is someone dressed like you doing in the woods this time of day?" The Prince replied he was on a mission to find the best food in the world and inquired of the woodcutter if he knew where he could find it.

"Sure," replied the woodcutter, "I can show you the best food in the world if you will help me chop trees and logs until noon." The Prince agreed and began doing the hardest work he had ever done in his life. He thought noon would never come and wondered why he had ever agreed to such a foolish arrangement; but his desire to find the ideal food overwhelmed his fatigue.

Soon it was lunchtime and the two men put away their tools and sat down beside a large oak tree. The woodcutter reached under a nearby log and pulled out a leather pouch and a jug. The jug was filled with water that he offered first to his guest before taking a large drink himself. From the leather pouch the woodcutter pulled out a large loaf of dry brown bread. He gave the Prince a large helping of bread that the Prince quickly ate before asking for more. This process was repeated once more before the Prince finally took another large gulp of water and rose to thank the woodcutter. "You were *right, that has to be the best food in the world," replied the Prince. "Today I will return to the castle and announce to the chefs and cooks that I have found the best food in the world."*

The first time I heard this story was from my third grade reading book. As a third grader, I had no idea what the story meant and shared my opinion with another classmate who also thought it was perhaps the dumbest story we both had ever heard. Years went by before I recalled the story and began to understand it.

For the first time in his life, the Prince had experienced deep gnawing hunger. The dry brown bread satisfied that hunger. Prior to this experience, the Prince had never eaten to satisfy a hunger and never realized that something so simple and readily available could satisfy. This lesson can be applied to wisdom if you are willing to put forth an effort to create the kind of hunger the Prince experienced with the woodcutter. In his early years the Prince had nothing to do and never created a physical hunger. His desire to find the best food in the world was just a mere wish until he experienced real hunger.

Looking deeper into this story, the wise will recognize three elements they encounter in their search for wisdom. First comes the vision. The vision gives clarity as to exactly what is desired. The vision cannot be vague. You cannot focus on a vision that is unclear. To the wise, wisdom is always their vision. To the

Prince, finding the best food was his vision.

The second element is the circumstance that creates the hunger. For the wise, hunger for wisdom is created when the desire for a more enlightened life becomes so strong all else is secondary. This usually starts when the wise become restless, unfulfilled or unsatisfied with current circumstances. At this point they struggle to seek those who are leading the kind of life they themselves desire. Realizing that adversity and consequence has created an awakening for a better life, they willingly follow the words and actions of the masters (those who are wiser). For the Prince his search started with his not being satisfied with the foods he had tried and felt there was something better and more satisfying. Little did he know before he would find it, a deep gnawing hunger had to be created. Since foods satisfy a physical hunger instead of spiritual hunger, he had to hunger physically. This he did by working for the first time in his life. In the woodcutter he found someone who had himself experienced physical hunger by hard work and who knew how to satisfy it. The same principal applies in spiritual matters. Once a hunger for spiritual enlightenment reaches its peak, satisfaction is certain.

The third element to this story deals with the masters who guide those seeking wisdom as the woodcutter guided the Prince in seeking his vision. The masters in wisdom guide seekers of wisdom by their own example. They never ask others to do those things they themselves would not do. They know some of these tasks are going to be difficult but never encourage shortcuts. Their message is perseverance and courage. Likewise, the woodcutter never asked the Prince to do anything he was not already doing.

Neither the master nor the woodcutter gives their subjects a shortcut, but instead encourages persistence with the promise of a reward. The reward they promise is not an idle wish, but one that is assured.

The final encounter for the seeker of wisdom is to stand before the wise and hear them say, "We have nothing else to tell you. You have learned well. Go, be an example to others, encouraging them to create their own hunger and always follow the path of the wise. You who sought wisdom have now become wise and are ready to take on the sacred task of leading others." (*As a Man Thinketh*, James Allen, p. 64).

Chapter Thirteen
Black Roses

Where there is no vision, the people will perish . . .
—Proverbs 29:18 (King James Version)

Long ago and far away there was a small kingdom located in a green, peaceful valley. The kingdom was ruled by a benevolent King whose only concern was the welfare of his subjects. He gained popularity with the people of the kingdom by making frequent visits to many of their special events and celebrations, which he even hosted at times.

In the kingdom was an orphanage for homeless children sponsored and funded by the royal family themselves. Being a special project of the King, he always set aside a day in the spring to visit the orphanage, talk to the staff and get to know the children. Just before each visit the children would engage themselves in projects of arts and crafts to be judged by the King himself. Prizes would always be given to the children on the basis of originality and talent. Prizes usually consisted of different colored ribbons, certificates of recognition and even a couple of times in the past, an opportunity to be enrolled in the kingdom's finest school designed for training the most talented.

One particular day, a messenger arrived at the children's home with a message that the King would visit them on the last day of the following month. This caused quite a bit of excitement among the children and staff. They all began to plan for the King's visit by discussing what to wear and what to serve for lunch (which was always one of the highlights of his visit). Foremost in the minds of the children were the items to be presented for judging. The staff wisely encouraged the children not to present something just to please the King, but some special item that represented their own feelings and ideas.

As the special day drew near, each child started on his or her own special project intended to be unique and creative. Some drew pictures of happy people, others painted pictures of beautiful landscapes and still others created and drew colorful flowers. When time permitted, they spent time cleaning their rooms and getting together the clothes they would wear to greet their special guest. The staff spent most of their time polishing, cleaning and planning menus.

Finally the day of the King's visit arrived. Both the

children and staff were busy putting last minute touches on their projects and chores. At about mid-morning, a carriage arrived in front of the main building with the King and three of his closest aides. Everyone came out to meet them and each child was given the opportunity to give the King their own special greeting which often included a handful of assorted spring flowers. The greeting ceremony lasted quite a while before they finally entered the building.

Once inside, it became evident to the King that quite a bit of preparation had gone into preparing for his visit. The floors were more shiny than usual, the lamps were polished, the furniture was clean and polished and the rooms were neat and spotless. This is not to say the home was always less than clean, but after all this was a special day. There was an air of excitement and everyone felt this was going to be a very special visit, for each child knew they had done their best work to present before the King and his aides, who would assist in judging the projects. The children tried to pick out the most advantageous locations to display their arts and crafts. They looked for the exact right spot with the best lighting and atmosphere for their particular project soon to be judged. Even though judging was still a few hours away, competition among the children had begun.

Once the initial tour was completed, the royal

guests filed into the dining hall for lunch with the children and staff. The meal was simple and included foods that were commonly served each day. However, one could tell that special care had been made to use the best china and silverware for this occasion. The talk around the tables was happy and relaxed. During the meal the King had a chance to speak with each child and to discover something interesting about each one. Nothing could make the day more special than to have the King's full attention even for just a short moment.

Following the meal, everyone gathered to tour the areas where the arts and crafts were displayed for judging. Each child that participated in the contest stood beside their own entry and waited eagerly for the King to judge it. The headmaster of the school came forward to welcome the royal guests and to announce that the judging was ready to begin. The King then came forward and began to walk in front of each item, making notes as he passed. Once each item had been reviewed at a quick glance, he returned to each one for a more detailed review. More notes were taken as he talked to each child about what their selections meant to them. Judging continued for almost half an hour while anticipation among the participants was growing.

At last the first winner was revealed when the King asked one of his aides to attach the green ribbon for third place to the painting of a landscape. First and second place choices were more difficult and seemed to be taking more time. One painting in particular attracted more attention than all the others, so the judges continued to return back to it for another look. Standing beside the painting, the boy who created the entry was asked what the picture meant to him. This question made the other children laugh as it did the first time they saw it several days before.

The boy explained that it was a picture of black roses. "Have you ever seen a black rose?" asked the King.

"No, but since there are no black roses, I wanted to show everyone how beautiful they could be," replied the boy. He further added that he hoped someone would try to grow them and share their beauty.

The King at that point asked for the blue ribbon to pin on the painting titled "Black Roses." Putting his arm around the shoulder of the young winner, the King spoke to those present saying, "Because of what this painting represents, I am giving it first prize and will give it a place of honor in my palace. The young artist shows promise because he is able to see beauty in that which is not but could be. The world and this kingdom need men and women who can convert their own visions into reality. Suffering humanity is crying out for those who can see beauty and goodness in that which is not but could be. Vision is the first step in creating a better and more beautiful world. Those with vision of what could be are often ridiculed for their original ideas, but with resolve and discipline they make the world better, even for the scoffers."

After making these remarks, the King then honored one more child by giving her a red ribbon for her drawing of people working together and helping each other. All the children then came forward to congratulate the winners, especially the boy who would soon go to the palace to hang his painting in a special place of honor. In the eyes of the children and staff there were only three winners; but the King knew there were more. He knew that everyone was a winner when young men and women with vision are discovered and encouraged.

Chapter Fourteen
My Story

At the completion of these preceding chapters on wisdom, the few people I shared them with urged me to include a final chapter telling my own story and experiences. They wanted to know if I considered myself wise. My answer: "No, I do not." Gauging my progress by those wise people I met in these endeavors, I am just a beginner in my journey to wisdom. The truly wise would give the same answer knowing there are always higher and nobler standards to achieve. Also, their humility and awareness would never allow them to admit they had already achieved wisdom. Anyone who admits they are wise most likely are not. So, if you will forgive me for not being wise, I hope my experiences often using the wisdom of others will encourage you to seek wisdom as your top priority.

I grew up on my grandfather's farm beginning at about age two, after my mother and father divorced. My brother was a year younger than I when he, my mother and myself moved in with my grandparents. In addition to my grandfather and grandmother, there was a great aunt, an aunt and an uncle already living in the house, which was large and quite adequate. My mother worked outside the home while the others cared for me and my brother and all the farm chores. As I got older, I began doing my share of farm chores that didn't interfere with my schoolwork. Meanwhile, my brother at age five had surgery to remove half of one lung, which left him quite fragile for a number of years, and he was often behind in school. Shortly after that, my mother developed a heart condition that left me with the feeling I was supposed to be the strong one in our immediate family. She was out of work for a long time and felt bad for not doing her part for the family. My grandparents sensed this and came to our rescue. Today I look back to my grandfather (Jule) as the epitome of wisdom and compassion and to my grandmother (Emma) as my hero.

Life on the farm during the 1950s was good. We lived close enough to a medium sized city to enjoy all the benefits of urban life such as theaters, swimming pools, drive-in restaurants, pizza parlors and the ever popular drive-in movies. I shouldn't complain, but my only complaint is that I had more than I needed; not more than I wanted, of course. I didn't realize at the time how many sacrifices were made for me to live this type of lifestyle. I never lived in a house with a mortgage nor in a house where rent was due, and I never understood the economic dynamics of family life; even though I earned my own money by being a newspaper boy for two years and a student school bus driver in my junior and senior years of high school. It was not until I married that I began to realize the realities of financial responsibilities. My wife grew up in a family where these responsibilities were emphasized daily.

I met my wife through a high school girlfriend. Shortly after graduation from high school, I gave her (my future wife) a call and asked her out for a date. From the date of this writing, that was fifty years ago. Three and one-half years after that first date, we were married. When we married, I had two years of college and a draft board requirement to complete. She supported me through both of these endeavors. When I finally started my career, there were problems I did not expect. I never learned to handle competition. It was my wife and colleagues who taught me that the only person I needed to be in competition with was myself. I only needed to be better today than I was yesterday. My two children Rhonda and Ryan also taught me about life. When I finally grow up, I want to be like them! My son survived a severe burn at age two and handled it like a real champ. My daughter survived growing pains in the eighties much better than I could have.

Going back to fall of 1962, I asked my mother if she knew how I could find my father, who I had not seen since I was two years old. She gave me the name and address of an aunt who lived about thirty-five miles away. The next day I appeared at Aunt Gladys' front door and gave her quite a shock. She welcomed me with open arms, invited me to stay for dinner (she lived alone) and we talked into the night. From that contact, I met my father. We never became really close and never established a father/son relationship although we remained cordial and friendly. I was twenty-three at the time and too many years had passed. From this experience I received two valuable benefits. First, I got to know my uncles, aunts and cousins. Although I didn't have them in my childhood, I am blessed to have them in my life now. Today I stay in touch with cousins that live nearby, and we visit often. I have always been close to cousins on my mother's side of the family and cherish memories of my childhood with them. Amazing how much alike both families are!

The second lesson I learned from finding my father was that you can't let your fears stand in the way of something you feel has to eventually be done. The fear I faced in trying to reach my father, uncles, aunts and cousins was the possibility of total rejection or disappointment in what I would find. If that had been the case, could I have dealt with it as well as I did their acceptance? Yes, I could have, but it would perhaps have been more difficult. Rejection or acceptance—each of these contains its own valuable lesson. Caution! Finding a lost family after an adoption is more daunting than finding a family separated by divorce.

When I was thiry-two my family experienced one of the most tragic events that could strike a family. My brother (one year younger than myself) was robbed, beaten and murdered. Within the next year, we had to endure the capture, arrest and trial of three teenage boys. They were found guilty and are serving life sentences. My mother never emotionally recovered from this tragedy. We were all victims, including his two sons, ages six and eight. It was at this time I adopted one of my axioms of wisdom which states: "Becoming a victim is a tragedy, choosing to remain a victim is a self imposed curse." I was the one in my family that had to be strong, and I did my best to fill that role.

For the next twenty years I experienced the usual ups and downs of life until at age fifty-two, I was diagnosed with cancer. It was detected in the summer and surgery was performed in November. Since my cancer at that time had not spread, a relatively new procedure was used, but it did not go well. It was more than a year before my body functions were restored and the pain subsided. Maintaining my career during that period was difficult.

It was then that I met a counselor from Duke Medical Center who became interested in my feelings towards what I was experiencing. She complimented me on my attitude and promised me if I would persist, wisdom would come my way in more abundance than I could ever imagine. I had already developed a strong interest in why some people gained wisdom and others never had a clue about what wisdom entailed, but her words accelerated my interest. It was at this juncture I began to realize that adversity was a teacher I never welcomed in, but now she stood in my midst ready to teach me valuable lessons. Without her (Adversity), I may have still been encouraged to write about wisdom but never in the depth I now experience. I saw too many others enduring physical pain, suffering and disappointments, and many of them seemed to be clinging to their woes with bitterness. I promised myself I would not give up. Since then I have become acutely aware that daily lessons do come from two teachers: consequence and adversity. Consequence, we invite in by our thought and actions; adversity, although not invited, brings with her gifts of wisdom. Through more surgery and radiation, I have remained steadfast and no longer consider my cancer a threat that will never leave me completely, but just a nuisance.

I will not trouble you further with details of my life, but the following example of how messages come to us from God should be of interest to you, the wisdom seeker. About six years ago, I began having the same dream over and over about owning a modest house with the usual average sized rooms. In my dream I was reasonably satisfied with the house until one day I went into a back room for the first time ever. Much to my amazement the room was large and filled with the most beautiful furniture I had ever seen. It had drapes and the walls were made with beautiful woodwork designs. Behind this room were other rooms just as elegant. Going through these rooms into the backyard, I encountered a very elegant patio with decorative black iron rails. The patio overlooked a spacious backyard with flowers, shrubs and shade trees as far as the eye could see. The frequency of having this same dream, although the details would vary slightly, was about three times a month for almost four years.

During those four years, my wife tried to encourage me to share my thoughts and understanding of wisdom with others through either writing or teaching. I did not agree with her, fearing that others might think my ideas and theories foolish. One morning at the breakfast table, I was sharing ideas with my wife about how to handle a delicate situation when she spoke up and said, "You have gifts and talents you never use, and you don't even know you have them. It's a shame to have assets that are never used or enjoyed." Those words were strong and timely. I knew at that moment what my dreams had been trying to tell me for years. I almost shouted out the words, "That's the answer to my dreams." That was two years ago and I haven't had that dream since. Once I learned the lesson there was no need to have it repeated.

Messages come to us in many forms, and when we allow self-interest and egos to rule, we miss the meaning. If we do miss the message or meaning, the messenger remains persistent and will repeat it over and over. THE KEY TO WISDOM IS TO KEEP LISTENING!!

Bibliography

Allen, James. *As a Man Thinketh*. New York: Grosset & Dunlap, 1939.

Danforth, William H., *I Dare You*. St. Louis: Danforth Foundation, Seventeenth edition, 1958.

Gibran, Kahlil. *The Prophet*. 1927. Fiftieth printing, New York: Alfred A. Knopf, 1979.

Haines, T.L., and L.W. Yaggy. *The Royal Path of Life* or *Aim and Aids to Success and Happiness.* Chicago. Western Publishing. Dickerson Brothers. Detroit, Michigan. T.K. Mills & Co. Cedar Rapids, Iowa. 1877.

Hill, Napoleon. *Think and Grow Rich*. Greenwich, Connecticut: Faucet Publishing, 1960.

Nightingale, Earl. *The Strangest Secret* (audio cassette). Chicago: Nightingale-Conant Corporation.

Packard, Vance Oakley. *The Status Seekers.* New York: Pocket Books, Cardinal Edition. 1959.

Rice, Tim. "Don't Cry for Me, Argentina," *Evita*. Los Angeles, California: Universal Music Publishing Group, 1976, 1977.